Road TALES

Narratives of Life, Intrigue, and Promise

S.J. Buxton

Foreword by Rev. Paul Price

Forrest Press

Published by Forrest Press
San Bernardino, CA

Road Tales
by
S. J. Buxton

San Bernardino, CA

Buxton, S. J.
Road tales : narratives of life, intrigue, and promise / S. J. Buxton ; foreword by Paul Price — 1st ed.
p. cm.
LCCN 2003091229
ISBN 0-9712410-1-5

1. Roads—Miscellanea. 2. Christian life. 3. Buxton, S. J. 4. Christian fiction, American. 5. Science fiction, American. 6. Bible—Study and teaching. I. Title

PS3602.U895N37 2003 818'.607
QBI33-1210

Printed in the United States of America

Printing and Design services: 7Dcreative.com

For additional copies contact:
Forrest Press
724 W. 26th St. San Bernardino, CA 92405
www.forrestpressusa.com

Price $12.95

To the preachers in my life.

They have marked well the roads for me.

Especially for:

my father, the late F. E. Forrest,

my husband, G. R. Buxton,

my eldest and youngest sons, Stephen and Andrew,

and to Michael,

who surely knows The Way

and who inevitably must walk there.

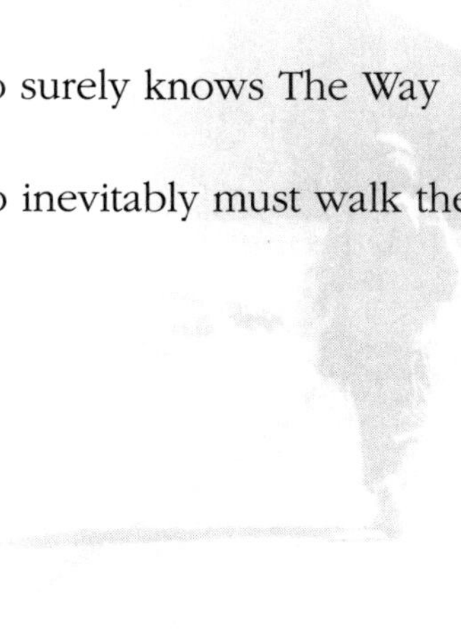

FOREWORD

It is amazing how our minds can be transported back in time to live again our childhood experiences. Shirley Buxton is a traveling guide who causes such an effect. I followed her through this book, seeing snapshots of her childhood, and her relationships with her father and others of her family. The book is such that it caused me to remember well the first fish I caught, the day I learned to swim, and the wonder of a quail's nest filled with eggs.

Sometimes she goes off into the wild blue yonder, and she may leave you wondering. Be patient: the mysterious trip will end, and you will be back on earth again.

The Buxtons are exciting people, and it has been a joy to know them. Their experiences and travels have often put us on our knees, but victory is a word they frequently use, because God **does** deliver them!!!

They have had great trials of suffering...BUT GOD!
They have had many close calls...BUT GOD!

To the Buxtons, I say: keep traveling, and keep writing.

—Rev. Paul Price, Napa, California

WHAT PEOPLE ARE SAYING

"My first book reads were biographical in genre. This genre became one of my favorites as I became engrossed in the lessons that I began to learn from the lives of others. *Road Tales* is biographical in its structure. It has captivated my mind and time as I have traveled life's roads through the lessons of the life of Shirley Buxton. This wonderful lady's vocabulary will paint a very poignant picture of the journey of life and is a masterpiece of art to be admired and repeatedly read. She has woven with her biographical chapters other interesting tales of fictional characters who might resemble your own life experiences. *Road Tales* will captivate your heart, mind and time. Read and enjoy her journey of life as you view your own road tales through the lens of her wonderful life experiences.

—B. J. Wilmoth, pastor, speaker

"*Road Tales* is a book of real life. As you read these pages you will laugh a little, you will cry a little, but through it all, you will understand that although everyone's road of life is unique, we all face some of the same trials and challenges. An enjoyable read.

—Jerry and Roffie Ensey, authors, speakers

“In each chapter of this book, the experiences Shirley relate keep you reading with interest and intrigue as you quickly follow her nostalgic reminiscing of former days and happenings. Her command of words is amazing. Also her instructive knowledge of the Word and her faith that God will see you through all circumstances is clearly portrayed.”

—M. A. Anderson, editor Reflections

“Shirley Buxton is a writer!!!”

—Etheleen Toole, McMinnville, Oregon

ACKNOWLEDGEMENTS

I must always begin with the Lord Jesus, who not only set me walking along the Road of Life, but who gave me New Life, when I was born again—of the water and of the Spirit. He is my center, my absolute reason for being.

My late parents are to be honored, for from my earliest days, they taught me the ways of God. They often walked a sacrificial road. I was too young to remember when they sold their possessions so they could go full time into "Gospel Work." But I recall my mother telling me in a non-complaining way how she felt the day that their meager furniture was sold and carted off by strangers. My parents pointed me in the right direction, saying, "Walk here."

I want to thank Betty Sue, who married my dad after my mother died, and who has been very dear and loving to me. She came into my life at a crucial time, and has been an incredibly positive influence on my life. She is a true Christian.

Jerry is an exceptional husband who has always thought me smarter than I really am, and who has encouraged me with my many projects. He has loved me to such extent that I feel truly cherished. His loving attitude has made for safe walking, and for some amazing Road Tales!

My own children have contributed in unique ways to my personal life's walk, and thus to the writing of this book. They are amazing, strong people and I dearly love each of them.

I bless every person who tended our family during those times when we tramped through rocky and muddy roads. Let me also acknowledge those who skip beside us as we traverse blissful and smooth paths.

Thanks go to each of you who has been so extremely complimentary about my writing, and thus have given me the courage to tackle this new project.

Special thanks go to those who took time to read this manuscript, and whose responses are included here: Paul Price, Jerry and Roffie Ensey, Melissa Anderson, and B. J. Wilmoth.

In Telluride, Colorado, my dear friend, Lavelta Stevenson, walked down that particular trail so I could take the picture that is now on the cover of this book. Thank you for that.

I cannot fail to thank Joyce Pierce, my friend of many years, who made helpful suggestions relating to this manuscript. Thanks also, to Sandi Richardson for assisting me with the final proofing.

I am extremely grateful to Clayton Brown, who helped me in a critical way during the concluding work on this book.

My neighbors, Lex and Lu Sensenbrenner, were a tremendous source of information and support as I delved into the mysteries of my new computer.

It would be impossible for me to write a book without the help of Rebecca Juarez. She has scrutinized every word, and kindly, but firmly, dealt with my love of long sentences and semi-colons, and with my absolute inability to understand commas!

Matt Jones and his crew at 7D Creative have taken my marks on paper and my blips on computer files, and turned them into a beautiful book. Thank you.

TABLE OF CONTENTS

PREFACE

This series has been brewing in my mind for some time, and finally it seems appropriate to set these thoughts to print. Travel and, subsequently, roads have been a significant part of my life for many years. I have seen much and learned a considerable amount: I have observed striking beauty and witnessed fearful horror. Serene and placid vistas have passed before me, as have indescribably tense moments when lowering clouds and raging storm obliterated my way.

There is entertainment on roads, and lessons are abundant. Sometimes, the teaching is obvious; on other occasions, it lurks in the shadows, and one must peer closely, or push aside the undergrowth, or blow away the fog to ferret out the learning.

Actually, travel and roads are a significant theme in every life and crucial decisions are demanded—the intended destination, the vehicle to get us there, and the speed at which we will move. Forcefully thrust into life, at once, the newborn is stepping along his road. The pages of his travel log may be many or few—who is to know? —but already the finger of life scribbles furiously as it begins the chronicle of his journey.

Some parts of this book are truths taken from Biblical accounts, and timely lessons are drawn. Others simply are the telling of a story—of something that has happened to me or to someone else; a lesson is not noted, these merely being here for entertainment. Are there lessons in those accounts too? You decide. The details in my childhood stories lack in absolute accuracy: although the stories are true, and I remember them and their essence well, sometimes the chronology escapes me. I ask your indulgence for chapter two. Plainly, it is fiction—I think. Read it carefully though, with thoughtful perception and with deliberate understanding. Reflect on it a while. One of my dearest friends analyzed that particular chapter and thought it did not belong in this book, and that, in fact, it is a child's story and should be presented as such. I think him to be wrong, and although it *is* a child's tale, I believe the story is much deeper than that, and thus, I have included it. He may be right though; if he is, rip out that part, and give it to your eight-year-old. (I ask a few people to read manuscripts, only a few, for it seems most people say something like "Oh, that is so wonderful," looking at me as though soon I will have a Pulitzer Prize in my possession. Knowing they are far from the mark, I choose only people that I know will be truthful with me. Then occasionally, as now, I ignore them.) Speaking again of the children, perhaps it is not a bad idea to read some of these stories to them: in particular, I am thinking of those concerning my childhood, believing them to be both entertaining and instructive. All of us know there is much negative and evil material in the marketplace, some of it directed to children. Carefully, we must guard what our young ones absorb, what enters their minds, and what plugs into their souls. Plato addressed that issue in his Republic, the most celebrated of his dialogues: "*...Anything received into the mind at that (young) age is likely to become indelible and unalterable; and therefore it is most important that the tales which the young first hear should be models of virtuous thoughts...*"[1]

Although for various reasons I questioned its inclusion, chapter five fairly begged to be written. When I considered cutting it from the manuscript, it stood on its heels and demanded a hearing. My hesitation toward this telling turns around the story's heavy sadness, and considers the possibility of inflicting new pain on Tim's immediate family. My dad, Tim's father, died a few years ago, so the issue was not with him. Neither was my ultimate thought for Tim's other siblings; rather, it was the feelings of Tim's mother, Betty Sue, that caused me concern. Having struggled with the decision, but finally deciding to include the account, I sent the finished manuscript to her. She would make the ultimate call. If the telling of Tim's story were too painful, it would not be included. She willingly assented.

Why study such an account at all? I recite Tim's history hoping that one reader or two may walk to a mirror and reckon with his or her own immortality. Tim did. A few weeks before he died, on his very short road, in his very temporal bed, his mother prayed with him until they were sure of his final destination. The Spirit of God filled the room, filled Tim's heart, and he spoke with tongues as the Spirit gave utterance, exactly as the Bible says. (See Acts 2:4, 38, and 39)

The mystique of unknown paths is ever with me. Eagerly I open the new map, its fresh road a promise of excitement and undiscovered opportunity, for who can tell what treasure lies around that bend, over the next hill, or across the broad waters?

Sometimes, I traverse a familiar way, and it is of particular joy and satisfaction to me. I know what comes next—the magnificent scene just beyond, that charming village in the deep valley, a placid lake, a roaring waterfall. In addition, I have learned where the chuckholes are and where the scenery is dismal. In his story, "The Most Dangerous Game," the author, Richard Connel, tells of engaging lights that lured the unwary sailor to treacherous shores where evil men awaited those who would follow false beams. I will not do that; I will not go after mistaken signals, for I have learned to avoid rocky stretches where danger lurks.

As the writing progressed, this book took unexpected reflective and introspective turns, and became less a travelogue than I had anticipated. The stories and studies commenced to describe an oblique curve toward the philosophical and the spiritual, well beyond the simple autobiographical sense I had envisioned.

Anew then, I considered the title *Road Tales*, a name chosen a long interval before I began the actual writing. After deliberation, though, it seems clear that the original title is the fitting one, that the name easily circles every chapter, and that the narratives in this book *are* stories about roads, be they actual or philosophical ones. Job spoke to the issue in his book, chapter 21, verse 29: "*Have ye not asked them that go by the way? And do ye not know their tokens,*" The journey of spiritual growth is long and sometimes arduous, one rarely smooth and seldom of level form. I do not presume to instruct, but rather hope that the sharing of these narratives will shed light on your way. My personal stories and insights are ones that truly I can tell, for uniquely they are mine. I trust this book is more than a smattering of words, but that I have permitted a glimpse into my heart and that by doing so, I have opened a door that will facilitate your looking into your own soul. We all are connected in some way, our common DNA spoken into existence by the Almighty, when at the earthly edge of time, God thundered, "LET THERE BE."

One thing I truly understand—I cannot find my own way; I know I must be led. This book has two aims: one is to acknowledge the Master Leader and His ways, the other merely is to provide enjoyable reading. Mark 8:23 records a powerful line that I believe describes our way. Speaking of Jesus, the scripture says, "*He took the blind man by the hand, and led him out of the town.*" In his little book, *Come Ye Apart*, J. R. Miller writes a beautiful poem that precisely expresses my sentiment about this subject.

"I do not try to see my way,
Before, behind, or left, or right;
I cannot tell what dangers gray
Do haunt my steps, nor at what height
Above the sea my path doth wind:
For I am blind.
"Yet not without a guide I wend
My unseen way, by day, by night;
Close by my side there walks a Friend,
He sees my way before, behind,
Though I am blind."[2]

I hope you enjoy reading this book as much as I have reveled in living these moments and, subsequently, in writing about them. As you read, consider your own road, checking frequently its target, for it has been my observation that at times there are those who walk down an uncertain road, knowing it may not be the best one, but resolutely averting their heads, refusing to see the inevitable destination. No doubt, I have done that also: on occasion, I have surely walked with poorly placed feet. Nevertheless, I have been distinctly blessed, and ultimately, I did find the right way. My road has been an exciting one, and although it has taken unexpected turns and has gone in directions I had not anticipated—nor would I have chosen—it has been a good road, a delightful path. I have not tired of walking.

CHAPTER 1
I Sure Hope She Can

"Here, Shirley, you carry this last package, and put it into the car." Mother brushed a stray hair from her flushed face as she handed the parcel to me. I could hardly see over the top of the box as Mother held the door open against the cold wind, and gingerly, I walked across the ice-covered step near the door. Carefully, I peered around the tissue-covered present until I reached the car in the driveway. It was piled high, suitcases and packages stuffed into every available corner, but I found a spot, shoved the package in, then hesitated a minute wondering whether I would be caught if I peeled back the paper a little to peek. I looked toward the house, decided against the deed, backed fanny first out of the car, and then slammed the door shut. I loped back to the front door of the house where I paused for a minute, drew in a deep breath, then rounded my mouth to form a small oval that puffed out a cloud of frosty smoke.

The year was 1950, the town was Springfield, Missouri, and it was Christmas Eve. Our house was a modest one, actually, not even a whole house, but four rooms and a bath tacked onto the side of a storefront building. The other side, the storefront part, was the church. My dad had been the pastor for many years—as long as I could remember. Springfield is a beautiful town in the heart of the Ozark Mountains: actually, the mountains are not very high, and some would say they are merely hills. The surrounding rolling valleys and hills are covered with splendid trees; in the fall, they flare, blazing both the neighborhoods of the city and the acres of farmland that lie at its outskirts. Leaves cover the yards, and I recall many evenings when our entire family went outside to deal with them, wearing sweaters and carrying rakes. We drew the numerous leaves into large mounds, clearing the yard of its litter. Then, after the stacks were ready and we thought them high enough, we three children laid down our rakes and trotted to the edge of the yard, where, laughing and holding hands, we turned and ran the distance to jump onto the leafy hills. They crunched beneath us as we frolicked. Our parents watched from metal lawn chairs, springy chairs, each leg fashioned of a single piece of metal, bent so that it formed the letter S.

After a while, one of them would say, "Rake the piles back up, it's getting late." We did so, heaping them high. Then as we sat on the ground beside Mama, Daddy struck a match and lighted the pile, which became a roaring inferno, mesmerizing us. I don't remember any problems with stray fire, and pollution was an unknown word, although the acrid smoke made us cough and smarted our eyes. The delicious scent of burning leaves lingers yet in my memory. Each evening in the fall, we smelled the fragrance as the neighbors, too, mounded and flamed their leaves.

However, now the trees were bare, the air was frigid, and tomorrow would be Christmas. As I went inside the house, Daddy was rounding up everybody. "Okay, kids, are we all ready?" He pulled on his plaid overcoat, then set his felt hat jauntily on his slightly balded head. He bent to help Junior with his jacket buttons, then snapped the hat flap snugly around his ears. "Here's your pocketbook." He took Mama's purse off the table and handed it to her.

Mother took her coat from the rack and awkwardly stuck in one arm while she fumbled with her purse. She transferred her purse to the coated arm, then stretched to get in the other arm, but she could not, so she set the purse down. The edge of her coat dragged over the floor. Daddy reached over and helped pull the coat around her, arranging it on her shoulders. I watched as she lowered her head to fasten the buttons. It was a close fit.

"Getting a little tight, huh Mom?" Daddy teased her with an impish grin, then put one arm around her shoulders and squeezed her to him. Then he held her at arm length and scanned her face. "Do you feel all right, Beulah? Are you sure this trip won't be too much?"

"Oh, I'm fine," she assured him. She averted her head and gently pushed him away.

I watched from the corner of the room, and when she caught my eye, Mother said, "Go on now, Shirley, and tell Donna to get in the car. We're ready to go."

We finally pulled out of the driveway. In a few minutes, Donna leaned up and touched Daddy on the shoulder. "Are we almost there?"

"Now, don't start that, kids. We're only ten miles out of Springfield, and we have a six hour drive ahead of us."

It seemed days before we got there, but sometime just after dark, we pulled in front of Uncle Tad's house. It was a "shotgun" house—the rooms arranged one after the other straight through the middle—and it had never been painted. I didn't know anybody in Portageville that painted his house. Instead, they were left to weather, all gray and silver. Daddy barely had killed the engine when the front door opened, letting a yellow round of light into the black night. Uncle Tad and Aunt Dot pushed back the door and stood smiling. "You all come on in."

Donna and I bounded up the porch stairs, stretched high to give Uncle Tad and Aunt Dot a fierce hug, and then we pushed past the adult legs to find Barney and Eddie, our beloved cousins. Junior came in with Mama and Daddy.

Aunt Dot warmed up some supper for us, and Uncle Tad and Daddy carried the presents in from the car and placed them under the Christmas tree. The tree had tinsel on it, angel hair, a few glass ornaments, and one string of electric lights. Barney told Donna and me about Eddie going with him to the woods to find it, and about the bare spot that was turned to the corner. Aunt Dot wouldn't let Mama help with the dishes. "No, now Beulah, you just lay down on the couch. I'll do up the dishes." She covered Mama with a quilt and gave her a pillow.

Donna and I were to sleep in Barney and Eddie's room on army cots, and they let us dress first. Giggling, we ran into the frosty bedroom, stripped off our clothes, and put on the new pajamas that Mama had made for the trip. The wood floors were covered with linoleum and fairly cracked with the cold.

"Are you all finished up yet?" Barney asked as he pushed on the door.

"Come on in," Donna said, as she and I scooped up our clothes and stuffed them into the suitcase. Mama had said not to get our things scattered.

"Okay, we'll leave out, and you all get your pajamas on. Then we'll play. Do you have any Chinese checkers?" Hugging myself against the cold with my flanneled arms, I bossed my cousins.

Barney and Eddie took turns looking at each other and acted like they wanted to say something.

We closed the door and skittered into the living room. Uncle Tad threw big chunks of wood into the round stove. Its sides glowed fiercely, and it actually danced on the metal plate where it sat. We held our numbed fingers close, then our faces grew so scorched that we had to turn them sideways. After that, we turned our backsides around and got cold in the front.

Barney and Eddie crept into the front room, but they hung back and didn't come close to the stove. Each had put on a different shirt, and Barney wore old pants with a drawstring around the waist. Eddie had pulled on ragged blue jeans, faded into white, and now they sat together in the blue horsehair chair, their arms wrapped around their drawn-up knees. Their feet were bare and red.

I saw Mama look over at Daddy, and then she leaned up and said something to him. I tried, but I couldn't understand what she said.

"Well, Tad." My dad straightened up and bounced out of his chair. "What do you say we give all these youngins a present tonight?"

I held my breath, and I looked toward Donna. Never before had we opened presents on Christmas Eve. "Really, Daddy? Do you mean it?" Donna and I raced over and threw our arms around him.

"Okay, just a minute now. Yes, I think we'll have one present apiece tonight."

Barney and Eddie unwrapped their arms from their knees and pushed to the front of the chair, their feet dangling free.

"Ladies first." Daddy handed Donna and me identical flat packages. Barney and Eddie got presents alike too, but Junior's was a different shape. All the presents were wrapped in white tissue paper and tied with red curly ribbon. Mother had shown us how to pull the ribbon against the side of a scissors blade to make it curl.

Both Donna's package and mine held white slips that Mama had made, and Junior's box held a mechanical car. He went straight to Mama to have her wind it up. Barney and Eddie received heavy flannel pajamas, and they grinned shyly at each other and left them in the box. "Well, go on boys, and put them on," Daddy ordered cheerfully.

They scampered to their bedroom, and when they came back, they peered around the doorjamb first, then slipped in and again sat in the big chair. Eddie smoothed down the front of his pajamas as he sat back, and I noticed they had slicked down their hair with water.

We talked awhile, and we kids had just decided to play Chinese checkers when Uncle Tad said, "Okay kids, I think you'd better go to bed. Christmas will come faster when you're asleep."

We raced to the dark bedroom and jumped into the chilly beds. I stayed curled in a ball, not daring to stretch my feet into the cold. Such a stack of quilts was on me that I could hardly turn over.

A slice of light that slid under the door from the living room was the only break in the blackness of the bedroom. We lay in silence for a while, then we began whispering, and finally we were talking loudly and giggling. "You kids be quiet now, and get to sleep." Uncle Tad opened the door, and we blinked against the sudden rush of light.

"Okay, Daddy," Eddie said. We settled down as the door closed. Nobody said anything for a minute.

"We're going to have a new baby," Donna said suddenly from her cot.

"No, you're not. You're not either!" Barney exclaimed.

"Yes, we are, aren't we Shirley?" Donna persisted.

"You are not," Barney insisted. "Your mother's too old."

"No, she's not. Donna's right." I went on, not pausing for a reply. "Daddy told us. He talked to Donna and me and told us to help take care of Mama because she isn't feelin' good."

The room was quiet. "Is that why she's fat?" Eddie raised on one elbow to look at me. I could just make out his outline in the dark.

"I don't know. I guess so," I answered.

"Hey, do you think it's Christmas yet?" Barney sat straight up in bed. "Daddy." He raised his voice. "Has Santy Claus come yet?"

"No. You kids go to sleep now."

Before the trip, Donna and I had talked about Santa Claus and presents, and wisely, I asked, "The presents are in there already. Where do you think they came from?"

"Oh, be quiet," Eddie muttered, refusing to know.

"I know what, let's listen for the reindeer's paws, then we'll know for sure if there's a Santa," Donna suggested.

Suddenly, I awoke. I had a special feeling—something exciting was about to happen—what was it? Then I remembered. It was Christmas. Gray dawn rimmed the plastic curtains. I sat straight up. "Hey, kids. Wake up—it's Christmas!"

Mama wasn't there for our next Christmas, and the baby had been buried with her. It was a cold night in February when Daddy met us kids on the hospital steps. Aunt Bertie and Uncle Flynn had picked us up at home hoping to get us to the hospital before Mama died, but we didn't make it. Donna stamped in the snow when Daddy told us: "She's not here anymore, kids. She's gone to be with Jesus."

We got along all right, I guess. I was twelve then, Donna was ten, and Junior was seven. Different women came to keep house for us, but it didn't work out, so Donna and I started doing the housework and helping Daddy cook the meals. Daddy cooked our breakfast and got us off to school, and we were home only about an hour in the afternoon before he came home from work. We usually had fried chicken or pork chops for supper along with mashed potatoes and gravy, and peas or corn to go with it. Right after Mama died, Junior started stuttering, and Donna threw lots of temper tantrums. I tried to stay strong because I was the oldest, and I felt responsible for the house, but I was probably too bossy with my siblings, and we quarreled a lot.

However, by Christmas, we were feeling better and we had grown somewhat adjusted to living without Mama. The only thing was Daddy whistled "Abide with Me" a lot.

One evening about two weeks before Christmas, Daddy asked a lady across the street to come stay with us while he went to the square to shop. "Let us go with you, Daddy. We'll go into another part of the store while you buy the presents, and we promise we won't watch." We begged and danced around him.

"No, kids. Now you behave while I'm gone."

We played Monopoly or some such game, but soon we were bored, and then Mrs. Timms let us pop corn, and she made hot chocolate. About nine-thirty, we heard the familiar noise of our car as it stopped in the driveway, and racing to the front door, we opened it before Daddy got his hand on the doorknob outside. Smugly, he smiled, took off his felt hat, and pushed past the three of us as we pranced about.

"Where's the presents, Daddy?" Where'd you put them?"

"What presents? Now you youngins let me sit down." He leaned against the doorjamb and pulled off his galoshes. "Here, Shirley, put these up for me."

Junior ran to the front room window and looked out into the darkness. "Where's the presents, Daddy? Are they in the car?" He raced back to Daddy.

"Did you get me a white sweater?" Donna stood apart as she asked. Junior had climbed onto Daddy's lap and I sat beside him on the couch.

"Okay, I'll tell you what I got. Move over, Junior." Daddy settled Junior on the couch to free his hands. He nearly always made motions in the air while he talked. Mama used to say that he would not be able to talk at all if somebody tied down his hands. He straightened himself, pushed to the edge of the couch, and confidentially leaned toward us. Donna moved closer. He outstretched his left hand, and with the pointer finger on his right hand, he touched one left finger at a time. "I bought sa-pah." He touched each finger, and then announced the next. "Sa-pah, sa-pah, and sa-pah." He finished all the fingers.

He switched hands then, and with his left pointer named on his right hand, "Sa-pah, sa-pah, sa-pah, and sa-pah."

"Oh, Daddy, just tell us one thing," we begged.

"Now, you know you don't really want me to tell you. It would ruin Christmas if I told you what I bought." Daddy reached to hug us up against him, but Donna had moved too far away, and he couldn't reach her.

"Well, I sure hope you got me a white sweater. All the girls in fourth grade have one. I'm the only one who doesn't." Donna glared at him.

"Come here, Donna." Daddy looked at her.

She hesitated for a minute, then walked to Daddy and stood waiting before him. He pulled her down, set her on one of his knees, and bounced her up and down. "You're still my baby girl!" he declared.

"Oh, Daddy, I'm too big." She jerked herself away. I really think she was pleased though, but she sure had been acting uppity lately. Recently, I had heard Daddy talking to Aunt Bertie, and I think he was talking about Donna.

"Beulah always said she was a sensitive child, but sometimes I think she's just stubborn." He let out a breath and added, "She sure does need a mother, but…," he straightened himself, "I guess we'll manage." I couldn't hear what Aunt Bertie said back to him.

After supper the next night, we all walked up to the grocery market to buy our Christmas tree. I can't remember the name of the store, but it was on National Street, across from Tindale's drug store. (The main thing I remember about Tindale's drug store is that we bought Fudgsicles there in the summer and that they were frozen so hard our tongues would stick to them.) Every year we wanted a pine tree, but they were too expensive, Daddy said, so we always bought a cedar tree. The woods around Springfield were full of them, and I guess that's why they were cheaper.

"This one suit all of you?" Daddy stood one up and bounced it on the floor. Needles sprang out and added to the heavy cedar odor that filled the store already.

We dragged the tree home and spent the rest of the evening decorating it. Donna cut herself with the angel hair, and Junior dropped and broke some ornaments. But it looked pretty when we had finished, and Daddy let us plug in the lights for a while before we went to bed. We turned off the other lights in the house so we could admire the tree. Some of the Christmas bulbs were scratched and cast darts of white light as we stood around the tree. Donna sure does look pretty, I thought. She had a lift to her chin, and when something grand was around like the Christmas tree, she seemed to look past everything, and her eyes were shiny with a far-away look.

"Daddy, please take the presents out of the car trunk, and put them under the tree. It doesn't look right without presents," Donna pled three nights later.

"We promise we won't peek at them."

"Please, Daddy." Junior tugged at Daddy's arms.

"No, kids. I think it's better that I leave them locked in the trunk until Christmas. That way you won't be tempted to peek when I'm not here," Daddy decided.

But, by three days before Christmas, we had talked him into putting the presents under the tree. You could tell he was excited by the way he grinned as he carried them in and placed them under the tree. Some of the presents had come untaped, and Daddy pushed on them and pulled ribbons over the bare spots. Some had no ribbons on them at all, and a number of bows were twisted and mashed down. Daddy had wrapped them at his job. He bent over and straightened the pile, then stood back. "They sure look nice, don't they?"

Before Daddy got home the next day, all three of us sat in the living room looking at the tree and the presents. Junior walked to the tree. "I wonder which ones are mine."

"Now, don't you touch a thing," I said. "We promised we wouldn't."

"I was only going to see if I could read my name," Junior pouted.

"Well, you can't. Don't touch them."

"They sure are wrapped funny." Donna looked sidelong at me. "Mama wrapped them up prettier than that."

"I guess so," I agreed. "But men don't do fancy things like that." I defended Daddy.

"I guess not."

Donna walked to the tree. "They sure are not taped good, are they?" She pushed a few around and lifted the tags. "This one's mine."

"Leave those alone." I moved toward the tree. "Do you see any with my name on them?"

"Here, this one's yours." She picked one up and handed it to me.

"Donna, we really shouldn't hold them," I protested weakly.

Junior gaped.

I shook mine. "What in the world is that?"

"I don't know. Smell of it—maybe its chocolate covered cherries," Donna suggested.

I put the box to my nose, but I could smell nothing except paper. The wrapping had torn where it folded into a corner flap, and I stuck in my finger to enlarge the tear. I could see a spot of gray box inside. "Let's all open one present, Donna, then wrap them back up," I suggested importantly.

"Okay Shirley. You're the biggest. If you tell us to." Donna was smart.

Junior stared, wide-eyed, then opened his mouth. "Which one's mine?"

We opened every present under the tree. My heart pounded and my throat wouldn't swallow. Donna grew pale and shaky, but calmly, Junior ran his new car all over the floor. My hands trembled, and my legs shook as we opened and re-taped every package under the tree, rushing at the end because Daddy would be home any minute. My vision was blurred, and my hands were sweaty. The presents looked awful when we finished, and we sat subdued on the couch, not daring to look at each other.

"Junior, you'd better not tell," I threatened. I could hardly breathe.

"There he is. Daddy's home." Junior ran to the door.

At supper that night Daddy said, "You kids sure are quiet. I hope you're not getting sick right here two days before Christmas."

We kids had a secret conversation Christmas Eve night, and we agreed to act surprised when we opened our presents in the morning.

That was the worst Christmas I ever had. Donna and I got big shoulder strap purses. The other girls at school had short-handled purses made from leather bullet cases. You got them at the army surplus store, but I guess Daddy hadn't known we wanted that kind. He bought Donna an orange sweater and me a red one, along with some other things, and we tried to act excited.

After we admired our presents and gave Daddy the tie we bought him at Kresge's, Daddy leaned back and said, "Well, it's a good Christmas, huh kids? Do you like what you got?"

"Yes, Daddy, we sure do," we answered.

"Bring me the paper, Shirley, please." Daddy switched on the reading lamp near his chair. I pushed against the winter wind to open the front door. I picked the paper off the stoop, and after I took it to him, I sat down beside Donna on the couch. I was sick, absolutely sick, inside, and I think she didn't feel so well either. I could hear the clock ticking on the lamp table. Daddy peered around the corner of his paper. "You girls all right? You sure have been quiet lately."

"Yes, Daddy, we're just looking at our purses." I rubbed my hand slowly across mine.

"Okay, then." He returned to his paper.

I sat quietly on the couch with my head inclined toward my feet, my eyes surveying the patterned wool rug that covered the old floor. I kept my head tucked but raised my eyes hard to look across at Daddy. It hurt me to look at him.

The lamplight threw a yellow cast across his face, and his balding head looked shiny. He wore reading glasses, and they had slipped down on his nose. He raised his eyes over the newspaper and caught me peering at him. "What's the matter, Shirley? Is something wrong?" He put the newspaper down, walked to the couch, and sat between Donna and me, throwing one arm over each of our shoulders. "Come here, Junior."

Junior walked over and sat in Daddy's lap, and Daddy hugged us together. After a minute, he loosened his hold and released Donna and me. We leaned back on the couch, and Junior pushed his head against Daddy's chest. We just sat there for a minute. Nobody said anything, and we were kind of embarrassed-like. It sure was quiet. After a minute, I said, "That clock ticks real loud, doesn't it, Daddy?"

"Sure does, Shirley." He reached over and squeezed my arm.

It was awkwardly quiet again, then Donna said, "Daddy, can Mama see us now? Up in heaven, can they look down and see their little kids?"

I turned to look at Daddy. He drew in a slow breath, held it for a minute, and then spoke. "I don't know, Donna. Maybe she can…just maybe…maybe she can. I really don't know."

His eyes glistened.

It was the fifth Christmas after Jerry and I married that I told Daddy what we children had done that winter afternoon just before Christmas. Snow covered the entire town of Rockford, Illinois where Daddy lived then, and it was still snowing when we drove our car into the city limits. It had been three years since I had seen Daddy, and he had never seen either of our two boys. Michael lay asleep in his car bed, and Steve sat on my lap, snug in his footed sleeper.

Our car became stuck in the snow about half a block from Daddy's house. Jerry left me in the car with the boys while he went to the house to get help. I could see the house from where I sat in the car, and I watched as Jerry cautiously walked down the icy sidewalks and over the drifted snow. When the front door opened, I saw my dad come out and grab Jerry. Looking around, as Jerry gestured with his hands, I saw Daddy turn his gaze toward the car where I waited.

Suddenly, he pushed past Jerry, hurried down the porch steps, and started through the middle of the snowy street toward our stalled car. I saw him coming closer, his bare head balder than it had been previously, that jaunty step impeded only by the icy street. I never took my eyes off his approaching form, but felt beside me for the door handle and firmly pushed down to shove open the door. I gathered Steve in my arms and stumbled from the car, skidding down the middle of the street to meet my dad.

Jerry hurried a few steps behind Dad and went on to the car to get Michael. Daddy enveloped Steve and me in his arms, and we stood there for a minute, melded into one form in the street. I felt Daddy's chest heaving and knew stinging tears were running from my eyes and turning icy on my face. "Daddy, oh Daddy. I love you." I pushed back to get a good look at him.

Donna and Junior weren't there that Christmas. Junior was married and lived in West Virginia. Donna had changed her name to LaDonna, and we weren't exactly sure where she was.

Daddy had married a wonderful lady named Betty, and she and Jerry watched the boys that night while Daddy and I went to the store to buy some things. "Let's walk," I suggested as we left the house. We hadn't far to go, and we wore boots and heavy jackets. It had stopped snowing, but the streets hadn't been cleared, and the sidewalks were covered with three or four feet of snow. Few cars moved. We walked hand in hand down the middle of the street where traffic had packed the snow.

"We've had some good Christmases, Daddy, haven't we?" I turned toward him in the glow from the streetlights. As we neared the store, Christmas lights had been strung across the streets, and they painted red and blue and green streams across his face. "Remember that year we went to Portageville and Barney asked all night if it were Christmas yet?"

"I sure do, Shirley." Quietly, we walked on.

We could hear music from somewhere…silent night… holy night…

"Daddy." I tugged on his hand, and we stopped beneath the streetlight at the corner. "Remember the next year, after Mother had died and you stored the presents in the car trunk before you took them in the house."

Then I told him what we kids had done. He laughed and said, "You rascals." Again, we walked in silence. I was absorbed in my own thoughts, as I am sure he was in his.

"Daddy." I pulled him to a halt again. "Do you remember that Christmas day when Donna asked if Mama could look down out of heaven and see what her children were doing?"

"I do remember, Shirley." Daddy looked tenderly at me. "I do. And I hope she can—I sure do hope she can."

Around us, the snow fell again, while colored lights reflected on the icy sidewalks ahead. The carol continued...all is calm...all is bright.

CHAPTER 2

The Electronic Highway and the Fourth Estate

The bicycle Milko rode was the new one, the moon bike, his grandpa called it. Actually, it was a very old bike, pulled from the McElwain's barn, that he and Grandpa had fixed up. They removed the rust with naval jelly, and together they had chosen the paint color—moonglow blue. The paint was not known to glow, at least nothing on the paint chart mentioned those properties, although the word "glow" was in the name. Yet, when Marcus Paint and Body delivered the bike, there was a slight shimmer to its finish, a subtle glow that was obvious to everybody.

Grandpa was short, not just shriveled-up-old-age short, but short. All the family pictures proved that. He made up for his lack of height in many ways, one being his width, as he bulged quite a lot. Another thing was his magnificent face, a grand present to all who looked his way. In his childhood, he had been a cherub, and when he developed into a strikingly handsome young man, Grandma was quick to snag him. Now, in old age, his face was a study in splendid character. His head was an acorn; the top of his skull that stuck through the thin hair was shiny and brown from the sun. The hair that did remain had a bit of black mixed in with the gray, and it curled into a fringe that straggled around the circumference of his noble head. He wasn't bald in the front but had bangs which he parted in the middle and that danced around and fluttered. Sometimes, he wore a straw hat that was exactly like an acorn crown. His wiring was such that when he smiled, his eyes turned on as though a switch had been tripped. He crinkled.

Milko was the last grandchild, so late and so far down the family tree that the great grandchildren were his playmates. He was a miniature of Grandpa, and perhaps because of that, or maybe because by the time Milko was born Grandpa was too old to have a job—whatever the reason—they spent lots of time with each other. They were firm friends.

Now, Milko rode the moon bike straight down the graveled road—alone. It was summer, and the days were long, but this would be the last ride of the day, for it was late and shadows stretched. It was the darkening hour. Crickets played their legs, giving out a loud concerto, insects buzzed, and fireflies blinked over the meadows. He rode fast, throwing up dust and small rocks.

Suddenly, he skidded sideways, and the handlebars were wrenched from his hands. He felt himself flung through the air: his body turned rapidly, and he became enclosed in a square space of silence and light. The crickets hushed, their music finished. He landed in the weeds, fluttering down as a feather from a fallen bird, and as he lifted his head to look around, he felt no pain. He heard a faint whirring, and looking in the direction of the sound, he saw his bicycle still moving and traveling upwards. The pedals continued to turn, and the bicycle jetted skyward at a steep angle. He watched with halfhearted fascination, a slight wonder penetrating his brain.

He continued to gawk at the sky until his attention was diverted to a glow that seemed to emanate from weeds not far from where he sat. He rose easily, then walked to the glowing place, and there he saw what appeared to be his grandpa's laptop computer. He lifted it from the ground, and the computer opened of its own power, spreading itself as wings. Suddenly, the computer moved from his hands and slid right under Milko's jeans, so that Milko found himself seated on Grandpa's laptop, suspended in midair. He was comfortable, and in a cool way gazed around. He lifted his head, and far in the distance, beside the sliver of moon that showed in the summer sky, was his bicycle. He watched as the bike moved ever closer to the moon, then finally was engulfed within the glowing planet itself.

The computer began to move, lifting straight into the black sky. Bright beams flooded from the underside of the computer, making the countryside clearly visible. As Milko sailed higher, he identified his own town, the small stream where he had fished in the morning, and then he recognized Grandpa's farm and saw that Grandma was in the backyard searching for him. He should have been home long ago. He watched as she cupped her hand about her mouth and called. Ragged streams of his name drifted to him…kooooo…mil…ooo. He watched silently, making no effort to answer.

Yet higher he went, and now the Sierras were directly beneath him, although he did not recognize the mountain chain as such. The higher peaks were pristine, covered with blue-white snow. Rivers roared over gigantic boulders, and although Milko could no longer hear sounds from the earth, he still could see clearly. He watched the mighty river, as its boiling foam spent itself, then fingered out into stretches of placid, blue lakes.

Turning his attention from the earth, he lifted his eyes and gazed straight ahead. Suddenly, a huge mountain loomed before him. The computer slowed of its own mind. Then, as though sliced through with a gigantic cleaver, the side of the mountain opened, top to bottom, so that its insides were visible. The mountain was in layers, and the activities within were clearly visible. Walking around within the bottom layer were a girl named Alice and a small boy who wore glasses. Hobbits ran beside the children's legs. It was a cheerful scene, and sounds of their laughter reached Milko's ears.

The computer flew on, entering the mountain at the fourth level, not stopping, but flying deep into the interior. Now, smoke began to surround Milko, so that he coughed and rubbed his eyes. The smoke thickened, and ahead of him, he saw flashes of flame and heard what seemed to be the crash of cars or other machinery. He detected the reverberating noise of cannons, and finally he understood that just ahead of him a war was being fought.

The computer stopped and hung in mid-air. Suddenly, he was jerked up by his collar as the laptop skittered sideways and flew away. He turned to face his captor.

The creature that held him appeared to be some sort of man who was very tall; Milko took him to be eight feet or more. His torso and limbs looked normal except for their size, but the distinct difference was his hideous face. The eyes were orange and had a flaming quality, set beneath heavy brows of a straw-like material. His hair seemed identical to his eyebrows, thick and heavy on his large head. His skin was yellow and had a stiff appearance. His nose was large, and each nostril was slit, the cut extending into the face, making visible a part of his facial bones. His appalling lips were lime green, between which showed his teeth—tiny and brown, but perfectly formed and evenly spaced.

The creature wore a red tee shirt. Across the front were written the words SOUL HUNTER. He set Milko down onto the ground, or whatever that was under their feet.

It was strange. Until this very moment of what surely was a highly unusual adventure, Milko had not been at all afraid. It was as though his rational mind had been snapped off and another mind had been fastened on. When he saw his bike fly to the moon, and when he felt himself being transported by way of his grandpa's laptop, it was as though he were merely an observer. Anyone at all reasonable would declare this to be a very unusual situation, and yet, to Milko, it had seemed ordinary. Interesting? Yes, it was interesting. However, it was also interesting to wade streams, to cast for fish, and to climb high into trees. It had seemed the same to him.

Now, though, his senses were returning, and a wild and frantic awareness of something totally gone wrong enveloped him. Beneath his thin shirt, he felt his heart pound. His knew his mouth was twitching, and when he tried to swallow, it felt as though an old cloth were stuffed down his throat. What was going on? Where was he?

Milko's legs buckled slightly as he was released onto the ground. He caught his balance and looked up as the creature began to speak.

The man's voice was a surprise—smooth, deep, and pleasant. "Welcome," he spoke to Milko. "Welcome to the land of Tpyge, to the Fourth Estate."

As Milko watched, the ghastly face changed, smoothing out until it was pleasant, and the creature became a very tall, fairly nice looking man. The strange colors had faded: the green lips were now pink, his eyes were amber, and his hair was a regular blond color. Only the small, brown teeth remained as from the beginning.

"Welcome," again he said, his hand still extended.

Milko had stood riveted, staring at the man during the transformation process. Now, Milko put out his hand also. The hand he shook felt cold and bloodless, lying limp in Milko's hot, small hand.

"Thank you. Where am I? What's the name of this place again?"

"Tpyge. The people here are called Tpygians. My name is Elom, and I know yours to be Milko."

He stared at the small boy, and then spoke again. "You do understand that you are a prisoner, do you not?" His smile edged over, showing his full set of small, brown teeth that had moved sideways to stay with his grinning lips.

Distinctly, Milko felt a cool breeze circle him, beginning just over his head and swirling around his entire body. A fearsome dread wrapped him, as does a garment pulled tightly.

Milko started his legs and ran.

Elom was not expecting this, and Milko had covered some distance before Elom caught him. He reached out his long arms, lifted Milko by the collar, then held Milko directly before his face. His strength was incredible and unearthly. "Don't do that again, boy." He threw Milko to the ground.

Suddenly, there was a platoon of men who stood about Elom. They seemed to be normal, except that, like Elom, they had mouths that moved sideways when they grinned their sick and fearsome smiles. As Elom, they wore red shirts with the words emblazoned across the front: SOUL HUNTERS. "To the caves," Elom ordered, and they all began to walk. Milko was in the middle and there was nothing he could do except to move with them.

In the distance, the sound of battle grew louder. Milko continued to smell smoke and what he took to be burnt gunpowder. They marched to the battle scene, its noise increasing. There were fires everywhere, and the heat intensified as they drew closer. Finally, they stood at the edge of the battlefield, and Milko gazed with fascination, though he was nearly unconscious with fear. He had never seen an actual battle before. Chariots jostled and cannons roared. He saw snipers shoot, then dash behind buildings; he watched an archer lift his massive bow and then release a deadly arrow. Milko's eyes were now of such quality that he could follow the trajectory of the missile exactly. He saw the recipient, a young soldier whose eyes widened as the arrow split his chest. The young man fell forward, and horses rushed over him.

Milko's captors had paused at the edge of the scene. Now they said, "Let's go." They ran across the battlefield, dragging Milko with them.

"Stop!" he screamed. "We'll be killed."

"Come on, kid," one of them roared. "You won't be hurt. Just keep moving."

At the cave, they halted and pushed in Milko. Inside, the head council spoke with Milko, glaring at him throughout the conversation. He was a prisoner, all right, in this strange land of Tpyge, and there were important rules he must know. They told him in an off-hand way that the country's regulations required that he be told there was a way out of the place. Almost no one, however, was ever able to discover the way. Frankly they admitted that absolutely nobody wanted to live on Tpyge, but pointed out again that few could find the way of escape. His captors would give no clues. The way out was thought to be hard, and should he find the escape route, it would be only through a supernatural force and his own perseverance. Once Elom smirked, his wet brown teeth and ugly lips sliding sideways as a unit. He hoped Milko would choose to join their ranks instead of trying to find his way out. Milko was known to be a bright boy, and they hoped to include him in their army expansion. He had four days. Either he found the way of escape by then, or he would be inducted into their army from which there would be no discharge.

They left, and Milko was alone. He looked around the cave and thought it not too bad; a cot had been provided, and white sheets were spread, along with a pillow. There were a bathroom, a chair, and a table.

Milko was exhausted, and without removing his clothes, he lay down on the bed. There were barred openings in the side part of the cave, placed so low that as he lay on his bed, Milko could see out. The windows looked over a deep valley. In the distance, he heard the sound of continuing battle. Finally, he slept.

In the morning, the bars across the front of the cave were opened, a breakfast tray was shoved at Milko, and the opening to the cave was left unguarded. He could leave the cave any time he wanted, but he must return by nightfall.

Never mind trying to escape by walking away, he was told. It will never work; there are guards at every street.

He walked throughout the entire day, almost never stopping, until his legs trembled from fatigue. Frantically, he tried to find the escape route. His brain seemed sluggish though, and he couldn't think clearly. Where was he? Where was home, and how would he get there? His captors were right about the guards; they were visible everywhere, and their eyes seemed anchored to him. It was really a strange place. Many other people were there, people who flurried around but who seemed not to see Milko. He must be invisible, he decided. Fights broke out frequently, and the people's faces were scarred. They walked with their eyes cast down, and many of them appeared to be sick. A large number were crippled; some were in wheelchairs, and others had heavy braces on their legs or walked with crutches. The air was dry and oppressive.

"Psst…"

Milko heard the sound and jerked his head in its direction.

"Psst. Over here. Here. In this store."

Milko walked to the building, an old storefront, and the proprietor summoned him inside. "New here, aren't you, son?" the man asked kindly.

"Yes. And I'm not even sure where I am. I really want to go home, but I don't know how to get there."

The man smiled, handed him a package, and whispered, "These tapes will explain everything to you. Don't let anyone know you have them. They will explain what is going on in this evil place and will teach you how to escape."

"How much are they?" Milko asked, although he was not sure whether he had any money or not.

"Oh, you can't buy them. They're free. But, you must listen carefully to the explanations and to the instructions.

They must be followed explicitly. Do not let Elom and his men see that you have the tapes."

Milko secreted the package in his clothing, and in the middle of the night, as he lay on his cot, he drew it forth and inserted the first tape into the player the man had provided. Included was a small speaker that he stuck under his pillow. What he heard was ghastly. These people were evil and were planning the overthrow of everything that was good and righteous. Their target was the earth, but it included every planet that was inhabited by anything good or by anyone worthy. The tapes contained escape instructions. A list of weapons was included, but although he thought he had listened carefully, he did not understand where to find the weapons. He rewound the main tape and listened again, but it was still unclear to him. He was afraid, but very tired, so he hid the tapes under his pillow, and fell asleep.

He wasn't sure how much later it was when he awoke. A sound had disturbed him. There, he heard it again—it was a scratching noise, soft, but continuous. He sat up on his cot, looked around the cave, and located the area from which the sound seemed to come. Creeping off the cot so as not to disturb the guard, Milko went to the back of the cave where he saw that the far wall narrowed into a tunnel. The sound seemed to come from its depths. He walked softly, trying to determine the source of the sound but seeing nothing. Thinking the sound might be coming from the other side of the cave wall, he rubbed his hand back and forth over the cold wall feeling for clues; perhaps there would be a crack or a line to signal another opening. He passed his hand over the wall down low, near his feet. Nothing. Suddenly, he felt a slight difference. There was a crack, a slight variation in the wall. He pushed a bit and felt the wall move under his hand. The sound ceased, and in through the small opening walked a lamb. Milko stared. The lamb wore a tiny keg around its neck, and somehow, Milko knew to remove the keg and open it. The lamb rubbed against his leg.

"Boy!—what are you doing?" The guard roared from the front of the cave.

"Ju…jus…just looking over everything. I couldn't sleep, and I've never stayed in a cave before. Just thought I'd look around." Milko stammered a reply.

"Get back in your bed. Stay here in the front within my line of vision. You are not to be trusted yet."

Milko returned to the cot and pulled covers over his head.

The next night, the same thing happened, and as before the lamb walked through the cave opening. This time Milko worked quickly, removed the keg, and pulled papers from inside it. The lamb stared solemnly.

Milko turned so that light from the front of the cave shined on the papers. As he read, his heart began to pound, and his head started to roar. *Choose two weapons from the following list.* A map was included, along with directions to the armory building. At the bottom of the list were these words: *THIS IS YOUR WAY OF ESCAPE.* The guard slept soundly and snored loudly. Milko felt his mouth grin as he climbed onto his cot. The lamb had gone back through the small opening.

When Milko went to bed the next night, he was extremely tired, but he willed himself to stay awake. He must escape from this horrid place, this country of Tpyge, and he had devised a plan. When he was free to roam the city throughout the day, there were guards everywhere, and he knew he could do little then. However, at night, only one person guarded the front of the cave, and he believed his chances for escape would be better then. The cave opened wide across the front, and a large barred gate was closed to guard Milko at night. Milko had studied it carefully and had observed that the gate did not fit snugly at the bottom. Milko believed he could enlarge that area so that his slight body could squeeze through. He needed something to dig with, and from the tape player, he had broken off the metal flap that housed the batteries. He would dig with that.

The guard fell asleep quickly. Stealthily, Milko dug into the dirt with his piece of metal, successfully enlarging the space. He wriggled his way under and was soon out on the street. He tiptoed past the sleeping guard. He must find the weapons cache so that he could arm himself. He ducked into a dark doorway and fished in his pocket for the map. The moon was bright, and he held the paper high so that he could read the directions. It should be easy to find, should be right down this street.

He located the building easily, noted the side door to be open, then slipped through the opening. He stood inside a cavernous warehouse with tall shelves that lined every side of the building, rearing high from floor to ceiling. He remembered the list of weapons and already knew which ones he would choose. He easily found the shelves where the rocks were, and he chose a smooth, white one. The harps were harder to find, but finally he located them, and he took the one he wanted. It was small and easily fit into his pocket.

He left the armory and continued down the street, thinking that he must quickly head back to the cave before the guard missed him. Then another warehouse caught his attention, for streaming from its slightly opened door was a bright light. He walked in and saw the warehouse to be filled with computers. One of the computers glowed, and looking closely, Milko determined that computer to be Grandpa's laptop. He looked furtively around, and seeing no one, nor hearing any noise, he grabbed the computer. Praying that the battery was still strong, Milko booted it up.

The screen lighted, the familiar tune played, and Milko was on-line. Furiously he typed in his grandpa's e-mail address and wrote: Help! I'm captured, a prisoner in this place called Tpyge. Rescue me, please!

Suddenly, sirens blared and giant strobes wiped the walls. Milko heard loud voices and frantically looked for some place to hide. "There he is," a familiar voice yelled, as Elom grabbed him from behind.

Milko was quick. He jerked from Elom's hand and ran. Elom was hot behind him, but Milko ran faster and pulled away from his pursuer. Through the dark streets he flew, but turning a corner, he found himself standing at the edge of a high bluff. Far below, he saw the battlefield where furious war still raged. Elom was sizzling behind him. Milko's head jerked in all directions, his eyes casting back and forth, as he desperately looked for another way. There was no place to go, and he determined that he would not be taken again by Elom; there was nothing to do but jump. The computer in his arms was a hindrance. What was he to do with it? With a frenzied motion, he jammed it against his belly and stuffed it into his jeans thinking it was awfully tight, but that was the best he could do.

"I love you everybody," he thought as he leaped into the black night. He fell through the air, his arms outstretched. His heart thundered in his chest; fear dried his throat. He tumbled, his arms flailing, faster and faster, his body gaining speed as it shot straight down. Suddenly, he felt a distinct jolt, and he perceived his speed to be slowing. Branches cracked around him, rough leaves swiped over his face, and he jerked to a stop. He raised his head, believing, but not absolutely sure, that he was still alive. He had set down in the branches of a tree. Far below him was the valley floor.

From the bluff's edge, Elom roared at him. "I'm coming for you boy."

Then with his very long arms, Elom swung out from a tree that had rooted onto the very edge of the bluff. He reminded Milko of an agile, angry gorilla. Milko clutched the branch where he sat, looking side to side, as he tried to think of a way to escape. He probably should jump again, but it was hundreds of feet to the valley, and somehow he lacked the nerve to fling himself from that tree. It surely would be his death. There was absolutely no place to hide, and Milko feared that Elom could easily reach him.

Within his pocket, Milko felt a warm glow. He thrust in his hand and drew out the white stone. Elom was in the next tree now, his wicked sideways mouth leering at Milko. In seconds, he would swing over into Milko's tree.

A scream to freeze hell wrenched from Milko's throat. "In the name of God," he roared. Simultaneously he lifted an arm, and with full force, he flung the rock. The rock jetted, veering and sizzling as it flew. Wham! It slammed into Elom's forehead, and Milko saw it embed itself into the yellow skin, then go deeper into the wicked skull. Without a sound, Elom toppled from the tree and crashed far below. On earth, the oceans surged.

Milko shook with fear. "I want my mama," he yelled. From his front pocket, he drew the tiny harp of God, and he began to strum, soothing himself with its music. Finally, he felt better, his courage returning.

Suddenly, though, he heard reverberating bellows, and looking again to the bluff, he saw hordes of the enemy army. SOUL HUNTERS, their red shirts proclaimed. They sneered at Milko, their vile clamors thundering over the chasm. Behind them, they dragged a flaming orange parachute. With their hairy arms, they flung it through the air and cast it over Milko. It encircled him, and they snapped its cords tight. They jerked with unthinkable strength, lurching Milko through the air, then finally they yanked him over the ground at the top of the cliff, growling and gurgling all the while. They marched off with him, shouting obscenities as they dragged him in the thin parachute. Finally, they came to a stockade sort of place in the center of town where they threw him inside.

Again, Milko was imprisoned, and as he lay on the ground where they threw him, he felt that he was near death. His throat was parched, his mind was racked with dread, and his body was bleeding and broken. Suddenly, the lamb was there, standing silently and solemnly, and, with trembling hands, Milko reached over and felt for the familiar keg. Within was a bottle whose label read, "Tears Mingled with Prayers." He tipped the bottle and drank, its contents slaking his thirst and calming his frantic mind.

He slept uneasily, fearful dreams tormenting him throughout the night. At first light, his captors shook him awake and yelled at him, "You're going to battle, boy. We gave you the opportunity to join ranks with us, but you betrayed us. Your time is here!"

They pushed ahead to the front lines where the battle raged around them. Milko's captors surrounded him so that he could not escape. Thick dust choked him, stirred up by the beating of the horses' hooves. He was mortally afraid and could not understand what was happening to him. What was going on? Who were these warriors? They jousted and parried, both sides furiously angry. Coarse howls vomited from their throats.

Milko was whipped from place to place, now knocked aside by a thrusting horse, then jerked here and there by the fighting men. He was thrown to the ground, then snatched upright by his captors.

All was lost, he knew now. There was no way out, no way of escape. He surely had failed, he thought, his body faltering as he was thrown about. He fell, and there he lay, his courage having leaked as from a tattered bag. Then he managed to stir himself, and trembling, he pulled to a sitting position. Unexpectedly, something surged through him, as if a gentle volt of electricity were circulating throughout his bloodstream. He heard a new sound, and at the same moment, sensed a shift in the battle. The sound was a peculiar one, a deep electronic clamor, and it seemed to be coming his way.

From a far stretch, Milko saw a column of light, the uncommon rumbling seeming to be connected to the light. The fused light and sound shafted downward, and where it touched, the armies fell aside, cannons tumbled, and frantic horses became entangled in their own gear.

The light came closer, and now Milko discerned that within the glitter was a man, the man completely ensconced in the beam. He flew to Milko, and Milko saw it to be Grandpa. His garment was a flowing robe, translucent white, whipping around his ankles, with the loose sleeves fluttering. His face glowed, as though a torch blazed through, and his eyes gleamed with excitement. The melded light and sound enveloped Milko now, and from deep within the mixture, he heard a supernatural voice saying, THIS IS THE SOUND OF GOING.

Grandpa scooped Milko from the ground and carried him in his arms as he ran. The light stayed with Milko and Grandpa, knocking the warriors violently to the ground as they moved across the countryside. However, as the light beam passed and moved on, the enemy roused, both men and beast, and began their pursuit of Grandpa and Milko.

"You're heavy," Grandpa said as he set Milko on the ground. Now they both ran for their lives. "Here, I'll take the computer," Grandpa said as Milko struggled to carry it. Milko heard Grandpa's breath coming in ragged jerks. They turned a corner, and Milko recognized the spot where, days before, he had entered the place, this Fourth Estate.

"Stop!" Grandpa ordered Milko.

They both stopped, and from inside Grandpa's flowing robe, he drew the laptop computer, which opened of its own accord, spreading itself as wings. At the same moment, they found themselves seated, mid-air, on its flat surface. Slowly, the computer began to move. However, the SOUL HUNTERS had turned the corner, well within sight, and probably within reach. They were virtually exploding with anger, the lead warrior thundering at the head of the mob. He was extremely tall, his long arms hanging nearly to his ankles. With profound horror, Milko calculated that he and Grandpa were within reach of this monster. White fear choked Milko. Then he thought of the harp of God, deep in his pocket, and although he still wasn't sure exactly how it worked, he dug it out. Holding it chest-level, he prepared to pluck its strings. The long arm of the warrior stretched out, and his hairy fingers grazed the edge of the computer. Frantically, Milko strummed his harp, yelling brutally all the while, and the warrior fell back. Slowly, the computer moved away.

Suddenly, the computer began to whirl, spinning faster and faster. Milko clenched his eyes tightly. His stomach felt sick. Milko felt as though he would surely fall. He grabbed the edge of the computer and screamed at Grandpa. "I can't hold on. Help me!"

"You'll be all right, Milko. You're fine. Just hold on. Hold on now. You're going to make it."

Then something strange happened. The edge of the computer that he clasped grew soft. The whirling stopped, and he opened his eyes. He looked to where his hand gripped the computer and saw that instead of a computer, his hand grasped another hand. Lifting his eyes, he looked into the face of his mother. Speechless, he turned his head and saw that he lay in a hospital bed, and that circling it were his family—his dad, Grandma, and Grandpa.

"What's going on? Where am I?"

The family took turns telling Milko about the concussion he had sustained during the bike accident, about the details of the ambulance that had been called into the countryside, and about the paramedics deciding to call in a helicopter. The helicopter had landed in the south meadow, and Milko had been airlifted into town where he had been here in the hospital and unconscious for three days. The doctors had been reassuring from the beginning though, telling the family all along that they thought Milko would be fine.

Milko blurted out the story of his trip to the Fourth Estate. They smiled, patted his head, and said he had been dreaming.

"No," he asserted. "It was not a dream. I really went there, and Grandpa went too. Didn't we Grandpa?"

Grandpa smiled in a peculiar way and made as though to speak, but at just that time, the nurse came in and said that everyone must leave. "These past few days have been rough ones for Milko. He has pulled through, all right, but now he must have lots of rest."

His family kissed him, promising to return tomorrow. Milko lay quietly in his bed, looking around the room and thinking—hard. That was not a dream I had. I am sure of it. Elom and those warriors were real.

Late that night, the nurse entered his room. "Are you awake, Milko? Your grandpa is here and insists on visiting with you."

Grandpa bounded into the room, his eyes glittering. "Brought you something, Milko, and I didn't want to wait until tomorrow." He took out a large package, obviously wrapped by Grandpa himself.

Milko eagerly opened the box and drew out three items, the first being a smooth white rock. "For your rock collection," Grandpa spoke quietly. "Rocks are good things to have." The second item was a harmonica. "There are directions with it. Thought you might learn to play a mouth harp while you recover." The third gift was a stuffed animal, a large one that stood two feet high. It was a lamb, woolly and firm, whose plastic eyes gazed solemnly at Milko. Milko looked at Grandpa and started to speak.

"Don't talk, Son. I promised the nurse I would stay only a minute. See you tomorrow." Grandpa smiled at Milko, winked an eye, and walked from the room.

Grandpa walked down the long corridor and through the front door. Outside, he crossed the lawn and stood beneath the lighted room which he knew to be Milko's. From the open window, a melodious sound wafted—the distinct sound of a harp. Grandpa knew its source to be another world.

CHAPTER 3
Dale and Taylor

As is true of most children, I suppose, I didn't analyze my childhood as I was living it, but looking back, I see that despite some negative and unfortunate situations, I was quite happy. We lived a simple life that revolved around our family and around the small church my dad pastored. The church, with our living quarters connected, sat on the corner of Dale and Taylor streets, its exact address being 1139 E. Dale, and for some reason, we often referred to our living there by its address, saying, "When we lived at Dale and Taylor..."

The church family consisted of fifty or sixty people, common folk like we; some lived in Springfield, and others lived in the country nearby. First United Pentecostal was the name of the church, and the services were lively, with lots of hand clapping, lusty singing, and powerful preaching. Brother Martin strummed the guitar, and a couple of different women played the piano, a beautiful upright instrument that was a player piano, although we never had any of the cylinders to make it play by itself. Actually, the piano belonged to our family, but Daddy placed it on the church side, for the church didn't own one, and I guess there was no need to have two pianos in that small building.

For a while, Donna and I took piano lessons from Mrs. Shaush who lived on the other side of town from us. Every Saturday, we rode a city bus to her place over on Cherry St., a fine two-story house with a little anteroom near the entrance where we sat as we waited our turn at the piano. Daddy had worked out a special deal for our lessons—seventy-five cents for both of us. When it was time for our lesson, Daddy would hand me three quarters and bus tokens or change for our fare, occasionally giving us two nickels extra so that we could buy candy or ice cream. One Saturday, we had extra pennies as we shopped in the drugstore where we waited to catch the bus after our lessons, and we decided to buy peanuts from a vending machine. By mistake, one of us inserted the bus fare dime instead of one of the pennies, and we were horrified, as we had no more money. Being too shy to mention it to the drugstore owner who probably could have opened the machine, or surely would have helped us, we set out walking. We walked down Boonville and across town to our home. (Although it was quite a distance for children to walk, the first time I visited Springfield after an absence of several years, I was amazed at how close the Square was to Commercial St. As a child, I thought of Boonville St., that connected those two areas as being many miles long, when actually, the two areas were not extremely far apart.)

Donna and I had to do our piano practicing in the church side of the storefront, of course, and that was fine during the summer and the mild parts of the year, but it was a problem, I assure you, during the winter. A coal stove heated the church, and a fire was built only for church services, so when it was piano practice time, we each put on a heavy coat, set ourselves down on the cold bench, and got on with learning to master the piano. In the dead of winter, we actually wore gloves to practice. This may explain why I am not a master pianist; otherwise, my playing would be of concert quality! These lessons lasted about a year, and I am grateful to my parents for the vision they had when they provided my sister and me this opportunity to learn a bit about music. I think it often was hard to scrape up the seventy-five cents, and they probably cried silent tears when they sent us into that cold church. Those lessons were truly a gift, for though I am far from being an accomplished musician, my simple playing of both the piano and the organ is a source of joy to me.

Often on Sunday afternoon, we children of the church would go home with another family. The Snow family lived in Strafford, ten miles or so out of Springfield, and I often visited there. The Snows had three boys and a girl, also named Shirley, who was close to my age. Samuel Snow was a pillar of the church, a handsome man with dark curly hair. In testimony service, he often concluded his talk by saying, "Pray for me that I will go the last smile of the way."

"Amen," the saints would respond as he sat down, an agreement, perhaps, that there were yet miles to go; surely some would be with smiles, others not.

Donna and I had straight, stringy hair, whose only curl was achieved by rag rollers. Mama would hold long strips of white cloth at scalp level, then she would twist the rags downward around each length of our pitiful hair, turn it at the bottom, then twist back to the top, and tie each one off. Our heads were then covered by dangling white sausages, a sight no doubt, but whose unwinding on Sunday morning produced long, bouncing curls. We tossed our heads and posed at the mirror. Usually, though, that was too much trouble, and we wore pigtails. I think my hair was more difficult to curl than Donna's was, for more old pictures show me with braids and hers with a ringlet or two.

Shirley Snow had chestnut brown, naturally curly hair. It was beautiful, and I envied it except when it was time for Sunday night church, and her mother sat Shirley between her knees and began to comb it. We had run all afternoon, so Shirley's beautiful hair was a nest of tangles, and she screeched as the mass was attacked with a stiff brush.

The Snows got their water from a spring down the hill from their house. Their house was much nicer than ours; it always seemed exceptionally fine to me, although it had no running water or inside plumbing, and ours did. I neglected to factor that in when I judged their house much better than ours. Sometime during those years, the Snows modernized their kitchen, and although they still had not piped water into the house, Sister Snow had a beautiful sink with built-in drain boards on either side. She proudly showed it off and referred to it as a "zinc," then a common nomenclature given to such an item, perhaps because many early sinks were made of a zinc compound.

Sister Snow made delicious pineapple upside down cakes, cooked in a black iron skillet. We children gathered around as she pulled one from the oven and then turned the cake onto a plate, the cake oozing with brown sugar glaze and showing the pineapple rounds that glistened with red cherry middles. I don't recall that my mom made cakes that much. She was a pie woman, and her pies were of such excellence that our school PTA often would ask her to make some for their special meetings. Her crust was flaky and delectable, and her coconut and chocolate cream fillings were studies in sugary bliss. Sometimes she let me stir the pot for a lemon pie, instructing me to watch for the moment when the starchy mixture reached the change-point and became glossy and translucent. Then she poured the hot blend into the golden pie shells she had baked. Atop each pie, she spooned sublime mounds of meringue, spreading the concoction evenly, then lifting the spoon in a quick plop to form meringue curls over the pie surface. She shoved them into the hot oven, minutes later drawing them forth, delicately browned pies. They were regal, worthy of the finest artist's eye, noble enough to serve from premium silver.

Among the highlights of our lives were the monthly fellowship meetings held from church to church within a fifty to sixty mile radius of Springfield. These meetings lasted all day and up into the evening with lots of preaching and singing. Around noon, the men went to the cars and took out baskets of food, and the mamas spread cloths and set out the food. Then we shared with each other. I loved those times, and have clear memories of my friends and me walking around with plates, gazing at the food and having a hard time making up our minds what to take. We called it "dinner on the ground," although it was not served on the ground but on tables fashioned from boards laid across sawhorses. Recently, my husband enlightened me, saying that the term was "dinner on the grounds." Surely, he is right, for that makes sense, but I am just as sure that we called it "dinner on the ground." At least I know I did.

My mom was a quiet, godly woman, and everyone spoke well of her. At times when we sensed God's presence especially close in our church, I could tell that God was talking to her, for she would close her eyes and put her hand to the side of her face in a certain way. I can see it to this moment. I was thrilled, although slightly frightened, when I knew that God was talking to my mother.

From the time of my birth, my parents taught me Bible stories and took me to Sunday school. I knew the Bible. I knew some things about the Bible better than others, though. I learned this one day when I was ten or eleven years old. One Sunday morning near Christmas, Bernice Kaisler taught our class about the birth of Jesus.

"What is a virgin?" I blurted out, truly not knowing. Her face flared, and her words knocked against each other, making clacking, disjointed sounds as she tried to answer. I couldn't understand a thing she said. A couple of the boys snickered.

I continued my quizzing, sure that all of us needed to understand this part of the Christmas story. "But what is a virgin?"

The teacher became more flustered by the second, her face so red that waves of heat seemed to emanate from her skin. Her faulty explanation baffled me, and finally, I said, "Well, was it good or bad to be a virgin?"

Today, it is hard to think a Sunday school teacher would have such difficulty in explaining the meaning of the word "virgin," but such was the case that Sunday morning. I'm not sure that I ever got it straight that day.

We were avid readers, although we kids had few books of our own. Every week or so, we went to the main library, the one over on Central St. near the middle of town. I recall the library as having wide marble steps leading to the entrance, with stone lions on either side positioned in a reclining mode, their paws stretched out in front of them. The library building has changed quite a bit, and I have been away from Springfield for many years. Recently, I mentioned those library lions to someone who also was familiar with the library building, and she said the library never had any lions. I definitely remember it as having lions. But she persisted and thought maybe I was thinking of a house on Benton St. that was close by and that did have stone lions out front. I don't know. Some day I'm going to check it out. Anyway, we went to the library, lioned or not, and loaded our arms with books. We also paid fines, for somehow we neglected to return the books when they were due. Once, I lost a book and was scared of the library for a while, that is, until I got the money together to pay for the mysteriously vanished tome. I don't know if I thought the librarian would send a policeman to my door or that someone would snatch me off the bus one Saturday in order to extract the price of that book. What a relief when I had paid the debt and again could stride up the central steps and check out more books.

Our neighbor across the street had the complete sets of Nancy Drew and Hardy Boys mysteries. They were stored in barrister bookshelves, each shelf having a glass door that opened upward, and I remember thinking that set of bookshelves to be one of the finest things I had ever seen. She only let us take one book at a time; we devoured that one, then returned for another. One Christmas, our parents gave a joint present to us three children—three books of our own. Two of the books were biographies, one of Douglas MacArthur, the other of Dwight Eisenhower, and the third book was a World War II account. We cherished those books, couldn't believe they belonged to us, and read them repeatedly. At the school library, I was especially attracted to a biographical series, green and orange books as I recall, that told fascinating stories of many great Americans. I believe I read every one of them. One of my favorite books was *The Boxcar Children*, a simple story of children who were orphaned and who subsequently lived in a deserted boxcar. Something about that intrigued me, and every year I read that book again. Laura Ingalls Wilder also entranced me as she wrote stories of her family and of their frontier life.

Donna and I had vivid imaginations, and we wrote many stories ourselves. Actually, they were plays, I suppose, and we acted them out as we did the supper dishes. Often, it took us hours to wash and dry the dishes for five people. My mom must have been the archetype of patience. Donna and I developed twenty or thirty sets of characters during our young lives. I wish we had written down those stories, for they would have been fun to read after all these years. They must not have been too impressive, and they certainly were not enduring, for I cannot recall any of them.

Sometimes Donna would look at me in a mysterious way and with a sly smile say, "Shirley, you are really not my sister."

"I'm not?"

"No, you're not. I live east of the sun and west of the moon."

In my heart, I knew she was teasing and living out a childhood fairy tale. But she seemed so serious, and she *was* always a bit different, and she was stunningly beautiful, and incredibly talented—sometimes she almost convinced me….

Although we lived in town, a country mentality pervaded our home; at least as far as putting up fruit for the winter was concerned. Every summer, the day came when Mama felt a certain urge, and she forthwith rounded up her children and herded us to the garage. The canning jars were stored there. The barren winter days had been warmed by cobblers and pies of such delectable essence that the cold itself had been stripped away. Now, in summer, the fruit jars sat on the shelves, empty as old women. A new stock must be laid by.

We tugged a galvanized tub to the backyard, then by the armloads we carried the jars there too. The fruit jars were dirty, some of them quartering thin-legged spiders whose existence we completely altered that afternoon as we tore out their gauzy webs and dashed away their filmy illusions. Occasionally, a mouse flashed across the floor, musty and gray, and we squealed as become children of a summer afternoon.

Mama poured steaming water and soap in the tub, and we set to scrubbing, the suds mounding as we thrust in our arms up to the shoulders. Before we were finished, our clothes would be drenched, but they would dry quickly in the hot sun. When the jars were thoroughly clean, Mama brought clear water, rinsing the vessels scrupulously until every trace of soap was gone. There, they glistened now; virgin girls lined up awaiting new fruit.

Our favorite fruit was blackberries, and our entire family worked to harvest enough berries for the canning Mother would do. We had friends who lived in the country near the small town of Diggins, which was twenty or thirty miles from Springfield, and they let us go onto their property to gather as many wild berries as we wanted. Picking blackberries is a hot, rather miserable job, for the springy limbs are thorned, set to guard the luscious fruit. We ate as we went, dust and all, so that at the day's end, our mouths and teeth were stained blue. Chiggers were the bane of the expedition, small itch-causing critters, almost invisible, with a ravenous appetite for warm summer blood sucked from hot children or from hot mamas and daddies. Redbugs, my Louisiana-born husband calls them, and that southern term is an accurate description, for if you can strain your eyes enough to see a chigger, indeed, it will be red. These days, mid-west and southern berry pickers slather on *Avon Skin-So-Soft*, or some other product with a high percentage of deet, so they may avoid the Lilliputian pests. We just clawed for days.

At home, we washed the berries in our galvanized tub, the water turning to ravishing violet ink. Then they were plopped into a big cooker, the finishing process determined by their ultimate form, whether canned as whole berries or cooked down and pectined into jelly or jam. At length, the chore was finished, the garage shelves scrubbed, then set with jars of gleaming wine-colored fruit.

Think on this:

Thick mitts grab the pan and pull it from a hot oven. Biscuits reside in the pan, tawny colored on top and as wrinkled as prunes. A plate is placed over the pan, the pan inverted and a round conglomerate of nestings grace the serving dish. One is taken to an individual plate where the morsel is slit, its insides showing powder white. A silver knife lobs on a mound of sweet, yellow butter, which immediately gives to streams and rivulets. Take one bite, plain.

Now the jewels are presented. Blackberry preserves quiver in the dish of heavy crystal. A silver spoon lifts the thick wine and deposits it within the golden stream of butter. (Never place the nectar directly onto the plate, for inevitably a drop will be sacrificed.) Open mouth and close down. Delectable.

Mama also canned peaches, but we skipped the picking stage and drove directly to the fruit stand. A properly canned peach is "just-so" firm but slightly on the soft side. The edge of the peach feathers out a bit in the jar, fluttering as does old lace. Halved, a perfect peach is its own goblet, a golden blush cupped to receive a fine dollop of cream.

A certain family was associated with our church but never attended any of the services. A special child had been born to them—my parents tenderly referred to him as a "water-head baby." His name was Sonny, and at first, I was mystified when I heard the adults say his mother had never held him, later understanding that the monstrous size of his head made it impossible for anyone to hold him. Mama and Daddy made calls on this family but had determined that we children were not to go. I wanted to, but Mama said, "No. You do not need to go there."

One evening, someone was moving a piano, and several of the men of the church were helping with the job. Daddy followed the truck in our car, and he let Donna and me go with him, while Junior stayed home with Mama. As the driver turned a corner, the truck leaned precariously, and the piano lurched free, crashing into the street. It was a predicament, as can be imagined, and someone had to make telephone calls. We were close to Sonny's house, so Daddy drove there, parked, and got out of the car.

Donna and I got out too and followed Daddy into the house. He was so taken up with the piano business that I'm not sure he recalled that we children had never seen Sonny. Anyway, I think it was Mother who was most concerned about the impression this would make on our young minds.

Sonny lay on a bed in the living room—a six-year-old child with perfectly formed torso, arms, and legs. From the neck down, he appeared to be normal. His head was gargantuan, a fifty inch globe, flattened on the bottom where it lay on the bed, turned sideways to look at us as we gawked at him. His eyes, nose, and mouth were positioned together, and were of normal proportions. His eyes were brown and returned our gaping stare.

My mom was right; it was a stunning blow to a juvenile mind, a rigid vision still etched into my now mature brain. I have seen other hydrocephalic children since then, but none with heads even approaching the massive size of Sonny's. An ugly door opened for me that night, a life size opening that stretched far down a dark hall where guttering candles flicker and where chilly air blows. I glimpsed dim shadows of the inevitable and had a momentary view of life's corridor of sadness and unpredictability: I grew up a bit that evening. When we left Sonny's house and went into the unlit night, I believe I had grasped a slight understanding of the treacherous human way and of my own vulnerability.

I was right in my insight of course, and today I understand even better. A slight aberration in the development of the embryo within my belly, and a "Sonny" comes forth, or a child with a twisted leg, a missing ear, or a muted mouth. At any moment, an imbalance of chemicals in my finely tuned body may change me into a raving maniac. The development of twists and tangles in my brain conceivably could take away memory, then my reasoning processes, and finally my most basic living skills.

Mercy is in order.

The James River is a better subject and some of my happiest days turn around its waters. First, I must tell of Uncle Flynn and Aunt Bertie for they and their children were often involved in our trips to the river. Uncle Flynn was my mother's brother, a good-looking, sweet-hearted man who was the epitome of neatness. The creases in his trousers were as sharp as the metal edge of a school ruler, the surface of his shoes glowed, and he would have preferred that even his underwear be ironed. Aunt Bertie worked as a waitress and got very little housework done. A blue platform rocker sat in their living room, and it was the receptacle for clothes newly brought in from the clothesline, or probably not so newly, for it was always heaped with un-ironed clothes. When my cousins wanted something to wear, they went to the chair, selected a piece, dragged out the iron and pressed the blouse, shirt, or pair of pants. Once Uncle Flynn called on the phone to tell me how he had cleaned their kitchen stove so that it gleamed and that he had polished the floor to a high luster. "You could eat off it, Shirley." Dog tired, Aunt Bertie came home from the restaurant and flung herself on the couch, not giving a rip about a clean stove.

Sometimes Uncle Flynn drank too much, and then he would come to our place, talk to Mama, and begin crying. He and Aunt Bertie were so different that they just could not get along. At one point in their lives, they divorced, later remarried each other, then divorced again. I believe they were in love but couldn't figure out how to handle their differences. Uncle Flynn never married again, but Aunt Bertie found a new husband and had a happy marriage that lasted many years.

Uncle Flynn was the first to die, and when Aunt Bertie heard he was near death, she went to the hospital, inquired for his room, and found her way there. As he passed over, it was she who sat beside him, tenderly holding his hand.

But, back to the James River. Uncle Flynn and Aunt Bertie had four children—three girls and one boy—and in many ways, we cousins were as close as any siblings could be. They moved around a lot but sometimes lived in Springfield, and we often saw them every day. Many Saturdays, our two families traveled to the James River and spent the entire day. The James River meanders around the Springfield area, and we had discovered two or three nice places where we could play in the river. Our favorite was a spot near Strafford, and after we parked and unloaded our cars, we set in for a day of fun in the water. We dashed into the water, cavorting and playing all day. Wild grapevines dangled along the riverbanks, making splendid swings. We grabbed those woody ropes, swung out as far as we dared, then, as wild monkeys, we yelled before plunging into the blue water.

There were two bridges at this site, one high over our heads, the other, an ancient one, at river level, with water rushing over its surface. Daddy and Uncle Flynn drove our cars onto the lower bridge, and we surrounded the cars, theoretically washing them but mostly splashing and flinging water.

In the early afternoon, the grownups built a fire and cooked for us: the menu was always the same—hamburgers. We were famished by then, and I recall those as being the best hamburgers I ever tasted.

Once a terrible storm swept through Missouri. The first time we went to our favorite spot on the river after that frightful storm, it was hard to recognize the place. The course of the river had changed completely, and our safe swimming holes were gone. Daddy went into the water first, testing the depth of the river and judging its safety before allowing us to plunge in.

Another time, we children wandered off a ways and went down into a part of the river that Daddy had not tested. I could not swim well at all, and I recall as we played around in that pool that I walked into a "drop-off" where the water was over my head. Frantically, I scrambled, almost making my way out, then again slipping in over my head. Finally, one of my cousins helped me, and we all got out. We sat silently on the bank, breathless and fearful, knowing we should not have been in the water there and saying little. Someone started throwing rocks into the water, and one of my cousins who sat beside me drew back her arm and slammed me in the head with her stone. I got up and went back to my mama and daddy.

I loved to walk on the river paths, and in my memory today, I can feel the dirt on my bare feet. Sifted and beaten down by centuries of people before me, the continual stepping had ground the paths into a pillowy softness. I pressed my toes into its easy warmth and meandered along as I eased my way through a blissful childhood.

"Time to go, kids," one of the parents would say in the early evening. We changed for the trip home, toweling dry if we were still wet and pulling on our clothes. We piled our things in the car and prepared to leave.

We would return, and waiting for me then, as now, would be the James River. It moved and gurgled, always the same, yet ever changing.

CHAPTER 4
The Mark of a Line

I took my first trip out of the United States in 1957. Jerry and I had moved to California, and my brother-in-law, Mac, took us to visit Tijuana, Mexico. What a startling experience this was for me, a young mid-western girl fresh from the gentle Ozark Mountains. We ate tacos at La Especial and had our pictures taken on a burro, striped, for some reason, to look like a zebra. The photographer gave us sombreros to wear as he posed us and then clicked the picture.

My most vivid memory of that trip was the line—the line that separated the United States from Mexico. Actually, I do not recall seeing the line, although I understand there is one there, and although I failed to see the actual mark, I realized that there were exact and firm confines. I certainly had a clear understanding that there was a line, a heavy, very significant one, an undeniable demarcation point between the two countries. It was obvious as we waited that day at the border. A string of checkpoint stations housed the Mexican agents who walked to each car and quizzed the driver. The line showed in their clothing; no two uniforms were the same, giving a rag-tag look to the men who popped in and out of the guardhouses. Overhead, the red and green flag of Mexico fluttered. (I compared their agents to the sleek highway patrol officers I had seen on California's extensive freeway system. As we left Mexico later in the day, we saw keen United States agents wearing identical uniforms as they stood near superior guardhouses. Majestically pulsating was the red, white, and blue.)

For now, the line continued to be revealed by the broken road beneath our car, the dusty view in my straight-ahead gaze, and the look of the ramshackle buildings that lined the rough streets. Slowly, we moved forward into Tijuana and fully began to know the mark of a line. This small marking in the pavement, this invisible line, as surely affected us as if a cement pointer waved in the air, telling us where to shop and eat, how to drive and park, what to think, and how to respond. The line flung inaudible words into the changed atmosphere, its fetid air assaulting our nostrils, decreeing a sense of vulnerability and of slight uneasiness. It proclaimed loudly: this is a new place, a different country, an altered environment.

Rutted streets jolted our car, and hot dust blew into our eyes. "Out of the way, Taco," Mac spoke to a dog at the edge of the street. "Don't see many dogs here, do you?" he teased us with a grin. (Earlier, he had lightly suggested that Tijuana's tasty tacos might contain meat other than that to which we were accustomed.) Nearby, flimsy huts trudged up the barren hills, and beautiful, brown children played beside the shacks. There was little grass, and I recall no plastic toys.

Haggling is the expected way of shopping in Mexico, and as we walked down Revolución St., the storeowners and clerks stood in the doorways urging us to come into their stores. They showed their wares, announcing them to be the finest and cheapest in town, and if we did not buy their items, they followed us down the street slashing their prices. Street vendors extended their arms to offer streams of thin chains, glittering as icicles. "Necklace for the lady? How about a bracelet?" Their heads sheltered by shawls, old women tapped our shoulders urging us to buy paper flowers. Disheveled mothers slouched on filthy steps and nursed their young, while dirty children pushed *Chiclets* on us, their little hands grimy from the day's business. Traffic roared, smoke belched from the buses, and strolling mariachis lifted their praise. It was a day in Tijuana; it was a day across The Line.

In Eden, God drew a line around a certain tree. "Don't eat of this one," He directed Adam. "The whole garden is yours—all of it—but respect this line."

Satan was listening. He took the line in his filthy hand and stretched it out, deformed it so that the tree was outside the line. "Won't hurt at all," he taunted Eve. "Go ahead. Take a bite."

Eve did. She took a bite, eating of the forbidden fruit, swindled by the disfigured words of Satan, deceived by the twisted line.

"Adam, darling, have a taste. Share with me," she said to her husband later.

"Of course, dear. I'll dine with you." And Adam, too, ate of the forbidden.

Lucifer looked on, vile and pernicious, a sneer slathered over his contemptible face. In his hand dangled the abused line. Pleased with his work, he threw down the line, and it snapped into place. In the evening, the voice of God called for His children, but sinful now and aware of their nakedness, they hid from Him.

The awful Line had been crossed.

When Andrew was three, we moved into a house with a swimming pool. The yard was fenced, but a sliding glass door opened our living room onto the pool deck. We kept the door locked, but knowing there would come a day when the lock would be forgotten, I repeatedly talked to Andrew about the door. "See this line? See here, Andrew, where the door slides. You are never, hear me, NEVER to walk over that line by yourself. Hear me, Andrew? I will spank you if you do."

"Yes, Mommy," my blond urchin agreed.

He loved the water, and from the first time he went into the pool, he could swim. It was a strange, unorthodox stroke, but he swam, as beneath the water, he humped up and down, propelling himself forward. Yet, I warned him, "Don't ever go out to the pool by yourself. Do not cross this line unless someone big is holding your hand." We kept the door locked. Often I would observe him standing at the door and looking at the pool. "Don't you ever walk out there by yourself," I frequently reminded him.

He obeyed me...until one day when the big kids were in the pool, and the door had been left ajar. He walked outside, stood on the deck, and watched the swimmers.

My heart stopped when I saw him. He was in no immediate danger, for had he fallen in, the big kids would have grabbed him. No, my heart stopped, for I knew he had lost respect for the line—the line he didn't understand, the one he didn't fear, the line he probably had forgotten—the deadly line.

I walked to him and firmly took his hand as I led him inside the house and began my line lecture. Immediately, he started crying, this innocent baby who truly could not reckon with what he had done and who had no understanding of the immediate danger involved; indeed, he had very little general understanding of pitfalls and of snares, of the fragility of life and of his own vulnerability. He was too young, too inexperienced, and unknowledgeable. Nevertheless, in fulfillment of my promise, and in hope of avoiding a catastrophe in the future, I swatted him soundly, finishing with the oft-repeated warning. "Don't cross that line, Andrew." (I can't remember what I did to the culprit who left the door open, but I'm sure I did plenty!)

So it is with us, us children and our Father. Sometimes we do not like lines, we may not understand lines, and frequently, we may forget about them. Perhaps we cannot even see them. It is conceivable that we take lines into our own hands, and occasionally, we stretch these lines to accommodate our activities. Perhaps it did not seem such a big deal for Eve to eat that peach or apple, or whatever it was.

However, lines matter to God—they are extremely important. If we are to please Him and truly to walk with Him, we too must understand lines; in fact, our understanding of this principle must reach into our very souls extending to such depth that a desire and a love for godly lines are created.

Lines are positive entities and must be acknowledged and respected, for without them, there is great confusion and danger. Indeed, lines are impossible to ignore. Try arranging music notes on the staff differently from the way the composer intended. Maybe up or down one line. Shouldn't matter much, you decide. Check it out. You will find clashing composition and a discordant sound that assaults the ear. Attempt a math problem with the numerals lined up at random in disregard for the line. Should not matter, again you say. A two is a two; a five is a five. Really? Change the setup of a division problem. Move the line over a ways, and see what happens. An accurate answer clearly is impossible. An airline pilot may decide to fly a different course from that assigned, slipping through the air on a contrary line. Should be okay, he decides. I don't see another plane around here. Everything looks clear to me. He moves that massive hull onto a defiled line, and all of us recognize the danger that lurks in what appears to be a cloudless, friendly sky. Faulty instrumentation can cause a pilot to become so disoriented that he may fly his plane upside down—and never be aware of it. Many times, a careless driver may defy a solid yellow line on a highway, feeling smug as he safely completes the maneuvers. Then one day, his timing slightly off, an unexpected car meets his head on, and a tragic accident occurs—all because a simple line was ignored. Lines declare us, revealing who we are: a distinctive Christian living in a city neighborhood is easily identified, as is the drunk who attempts to walk a straight line. Finally, lines are fixed for our safety, measuring out secure places.

What wise words David wrote in Psalm 16:6, "*The lines are fallen unto me in pleasant places;...*"

Consider the reach of Rahab's cord, a scarlet line that stretched to Calvary, and that by its symbolism encompassed water baptism in Jesus' name and the infilling of the Holy Ghost—salvation and regeneration. This astonishing account is told in the early chapters of Joshua. Moses had recently died, having led the Children of Israel throughout the wilderness for forty years and bringing them now to the brink of the river Jordan. Before his death, Moses laid his hands on Joshua and declared him his successor. Deuteronomy 34:9 says, "*...Joshua...was full of the spirit of wisdom...*"

Joshua was faced with a formidable task, that of taking the people over Jordan and of conquering the land of Canaan. It was harvest time; the raging river was completely out of its banks, and just beyond the river lay Jericho, the first town that must be conquered. Unquestionably, Joshua used all the tools available to him as he made a reconnaissance, selecting two men who were to slip into Jericho, assess the situation, and then return with a report. We are not told the names of the spies, but no doubt, they were among the finest of Joshua's men, strong and courageous. The spies slipped into Jericho and, at some point, found their way to Rahab's house, a house that Scripture plainly says was that of a harlot. It was an extraordinary situation, and it seems certain that God had prepared Rahab for the role she was to play. She invited in the spies, hid them among the stalks of flax on her rooftop, and when the king of Jericho sent his henchmen to rout out the spies, she calmly lied, denying they were still there. (Remember that she was a heathen, merely beginning to know God and His ways, only starting her conversion to Judaism.) "They were here earlier," she admitted to the king's men. "But I don't know where they are now. Perhaps if you hurry you will be able to apprehend them" (Joshua 2:1-7).

As the king's agents rushed to find the missing men, Rahab went to the spies hidden on her rooftop and revealed her godly affirmation. She admitted that she knew their God had given them the land and that all her people had heard of the miracles He had done for the Israelites. "*And as soon as we had heard these things, our hearts did melt, neither did there remain any more courage in any man, because of you: for the Lord your God, He is God in heaven above, and in earth beneath*" (Joshua 2:11). When Rahab began to plead for her life and for that of her family, the spies agreed that because she had saved them, they also would deal kindly with her and her family when the armies of Israel invaded Jericho.

Rahab took the spies to a window in her house and told them her plan for their escape. She took out a scarlet cord and demonstrated how the spies could descend on the rope, where they would set down outside the city wall.

Then the greatest part of this story is laid open, as in verses 18 and 19 the spies respond to Rahab and to her scarlet cord: "*Behold, when we come into the land, thou shalt bind this line of scarlet thread in the window which thou didst let us down by: and thou shalt bring thy father, and thy mother, and thy brethren, and all thy father's household, home unto thee...and whosoever shall be with thee in the house, his blood shall be on our head, if any hand be upon him.*"

Skip to chapter six. The Israelites invaded Jericho resulting in a resounding victory, verse 21 saying, "*And they utterly destroyed all that was in the city, both man and woman, young and old, and ox, and sheep, and ass, with the edge of the sword.*" But not so Rahab! Verse 23 tells of her exalted deliverance. "*And the young men that were spies went in, and brought out Rahab, and her father, and her mother, and her brethren, and all that she had; and they brought out all her kindred, and left them without the camp of Israel.*"

It was the line that effected this marvelous deliverance: it was the scarlet cord. Barnes Notes remark that scarlet was often used in the Levitical rites, especially in those connected with the idea of putting away of sin and its consequences.[3] Leviticus 14:4, 6, and 51 mention the use of scarlet in the cleansing of lepers, and Exodus 12:7 and 13 speak to sacrificial blood being applied during the Passover, thus preventing the death angel from branding that household. Rahab's cord or line was an emblem of salvation, signifying the blood of Jesus and its redeeming flow. The line separated Rahab from the people of Jericho, and that same line gathered her into the glories of God, even to such degree that Rahab became the mother of the line from which sprang David and eventually, Jesus Christ. Contemporary Bible commentator, Dr. Merrill Unger, says, "that the Rahab (Rachab KJV) mentioned by Matthew is Rahab the harlot is as certain as that David in the genealogy is the same person as David in the books of Samuel."[4] It is a remarkable story.

"*...and she bound the scarlet line in the window*" (Joshua 2:21).

A thin line shot over a vast chasm, in time becomes a bridge, its prime course built upon, thickened, and fortified. Extensive ranks are established, stout cables and twists of steel vault skyward until finally, the connection is achieved, and the mark of a line is laid. Wayfarers now may pass over.

Those of contemptuous attitude often condemn the principle of restrictions. Giddy with thought of vacuous freedom, they flit here and there having scant foundational beliefs. I was enlightened as in preparation for this chapter I made an in-depth study of an oft-quoted portion of scripture and learned of profound truths there that previously I had not understood. (It is another subject, I suppose, but I must say it now: Is not the Bible incredible? Its words, though read repeatedly, are yet fresh. The Bible is rejuvenating water that springs up with quickening and with sweet revelation.) Gripping discernment and, I believe, a holy awareness seized me as I studied the 28th chapter of Isaiah.

Verses 9 and 10 read thus: "*Whom shall he teach knowledge? And whom shall he make to understand doctrine? Them that are weaned from the milk, and drawn from the breasts. For precept must be upon precept, precept upon precept; line upon line, line upon line; here a little, and there a little:*" I have heard that scripture quoted for as long as I can remember, but the understanding that these words were spoken by scoffers, reputed to be drunken priests and false prophets, had eluded me. I consulted several commentaries and each agreed with the first. These men were mimicking the prophets as though they were teaching little children in a school. "Must you teach us so—line upon line? Must we be treated as children? Are we babies, barely weaned from the breast?"

Jamieson, Fausset, and Brown in their commentary make an interesting observation: "The repetition of sounds in Hebrew, *tzav, latzav, tzav latzav, qav laqav, qav laqav,* expresses the scorn of the imitators of Isaiah's speaking."[5]

Keil and Delitzsch say, "These words are intended to throw ridicule upon the smallness and vexatious character of the prophet's interminable and uninterrupted chidings."[6]

According to the *Companion Bible*, the Hebrew words translated into common English were actually a taunting rhyme: Law Upon Law—Saw Upon Saw.

Evidently, the prophet Isaiah listened to his jeering critics as they scoffed and slung insulting and sarcastic words that denounced not only Isaiah's teachings, but also those of the other prophets. For in response, Isaiah acknowledges the prophet's teaching to be as the scorners had said. The teaching was simple—line upon line, precept upon precept. In verse 13, he thunders, using many of their own words but adding a fateful pronouncement of the end of the wicked. "*But the word of the LORD was unto them precept upon precept, precept upon precept; line upon line, line upon line; here a little, and there a little; that they might go, and fall backward, and be broken, and snared, and taken.*" In verses 14 and 15, he blasts them: "*Wherefore hear the word of the LORD, ye scornful men, that rule this people which is in Jerusalem. Because ye have said, We have made a covenant with death, and with hell are we at agreement; when the overflowing scourge shall pass through, it shall not come unto us: for we have made lies our refuge, and under falsehood have we hid ourselves.*"

The Dean of Canterbury remarks on this verse in a commentary published in 1880 by the *Society for Promoting Christian Knowledge.* "The drunken priests and prophets had rightly described God's method of teaching. There is in the Bible a gentle urgency, ever pressing upon men the same great truths. So too the progress of true science is gradual, step by step; and in religion it is even more necessary to keep certain great fundamental principles ever in view. But the scornful rulers of Jerusalem wanted novelty. Their object was, not spiritual advancement, but the excitement and mental pleasure given by oratory. But in rejecting God's method of teaching, they ensured their own ruin.

There is great irony in the prophet's supposition that these rulers had made a private arrangement with the grim tyrant death. Nothing short of this could explain their conduct."

As a follower of Christ, I have an intense desire to walk carefully, attending to lines and paying attention to the teaching of pertinent precepts. After a while, I will inculcate them into my very soul. They will become part of me and finally—I truly believe it—finally, I will take on the blessed nature of Jesus. Many years ago, in my Bible, I underlined the second half of Isaiah 66:2. "*...but to this man will I* [the Lord] *look, even to him that is poor and of a contrite spirit, and trembleth at my word.*" Let me tremble when I hear the Word of God spoken, when I read its pages, and as God Himself speaks into my own ear. Let me not ignore His ministers or scoff at their words. Rather, let me eagerly hear from God and from His men, let me fervently study the crucial lines and carefully follow, so that my way will be blessed and ever upward.

"*But the word of the LORD was unto them...line upon line...*" (Isaiah 28:13).

In the early 1800s, the Natchez Trace became an important commercial and military route between Nashville, TN., and Natchez, MS. The road originally followed an historic Indian trace, or trail. Pioneers who floated their goods on flatboats down the Mississippi River to New Orleans often returned on horseback along this route. Settlers moving into Alabama, Florida, Louisiana, Mississippi, or Texas frequently traveled south on the Trace. Congress made it a post road in 1800. On May 18, 1938, the Natchez Trace Parkway was established and when completed will cover 444 miles of Parkway. As of October 2002, 423 miles of this highway had been completed. The Parkway preserves significant historical sites such as Emerald Mound, the second largest ceremonial mound in the United States, plantation sites, pioneer stands/inns, archeological sites/villages, pioneer and slave cemeteries and an historic housing site, part of the resettlement program of Franklin D. Roosevelt's "New Deal". The Trace tells the story of great leaders such as Meriwether Lewis and Andrew Jackson and of outlaws such as John Murrell and Samuel Mason.[7]

A few years ago, as my husband and I traveled there, we observed that for many miles along this splendid highway, the actual Natchez Trace is plainly visible. This prompted an interesting discussion between Jerry and me as we imagined the stories of the varied people who tramped through those wooded areas and who had pounded out the Trace, that faint but still visible line. Who were these people? What were their living habits? How did they look, dress, work, travel and eat? How did they worship? What sort of family lives did they have? What of their marriages, schools, and trading places?

The chronicle of these people actually does exist: recorded traditions, historical accounts of local culture and folklore, and the trail—the line their feet made. Our heads full of wonder and of imaginations, Jerry and I gazed at that path, straining our eyes to follow it, as sometimes it disappeared, no longer discernable, then back again it would be.

Once a line has been staked, although its principle structure may subsequently be removed, there always remains a trace, a mark, a line. In a church gone liberal may be seen a plain-faced grandmother or a beautiful young lady whose uncut hair hangs in a gloss down her back or is finely twisted into a graceful form.

(Author's note: I believe that many sincere people who read this book may be unfamiliar with the Biblical principle concerning the length of both men's and women's hair and that they may not realize the profound significance included in this teaching, and thus might be offended, or at the least confused, by the statements in the last paragraph. Since the thrust of this book is not to delve into that question, I considered eliminating these remarks. However, I felt a check in my spirit, reasoning that to be true to myself, and thus to you, the reader, I must include those remarks. The statements that follow in the next two paragraphs may also raise honest questions in your mind. Please contact me if that is the case, and I will do all I can to assist you in your search for full Biblical truth.)

In deserted prayer rooms may be heard the haunting cry of a single lonely being. Perhaps may be discovered a powerful church whose worship service proceeds quite nicely without benefit of disco lights and rock music. Perchance, a young soul may seize a faint, pure memory of the line. In the retrospection of a young father may clearly echo the admonition he heard so long ago, "*Wherefore, come out from among them, and be ye separate...*" (II Corinthians 6:17).

It could be possible to knock on the door and be fortunate enough to find a home without the sounds of "Hollywood," a home whose bookshelves and radio receivers are devoid of filth and lacking in vile language. My conviction that a large portion of TV programming is of a disgusting and debased nature, and has little redeeming value, was recently underscored by the following question and answer column in *Parade Magazine*:

Question: "From the Sopranos to CSI:Miami, TV characters are throwing up all over the place. Why is vomiting now so popular? —D.K., Madison, Wis.

Answer: Now that nudity, gore and foul language have become common nightly fare, TV writers are desperately searching for something with shock value. In our view, they are only succeeding in grossing out their audiences."[8]

These words become even more startling as one considers unlikely the *Parade Magazine* to be a bastion of conservative, religious thinking.

It lay before the man, rough but straight, and he allowed his calloused fingers the pleasure of rubbing across the promising surface. A familiar scent wafted into his nostrils. Carefully, he inspected the piece, gauged it, and then laid it aside.

It had begun as a seed, cast into the damp earth where its shell rotted. One springtime, the tree shot up. Through the years, it had flourished, drawing nutrients from the soil and through the veins in its leaves, finally maturing into a massive tree. Birds had nested there.

One day they call for the piece the man had stacked, and he takes it to them. They place it upon the ground, a board long and narrow, describing a line, a mark, an intrusion on the earth where it lies.

The crowd leads another man to the spot, and lifting it from the earth, the soldier thrusts the beam onto the man's back. Jesus bends low and takes up the cross.

On the way, He falters, and another is pressed to carry the load.

On the ridge of Golgotha, again they throw the piece to the ground, a mark, a simple line. There onto, Jesus is laid and hammered into place.

Groaning with strain, the soldiers lift the cross and with a jolt drop it into the deep hole.

There. Now it stands, the form silhouetted against the darkening Jerusalem sky. But there are three, you say. See, there are two more, one on either side of His. Yes, there are three. But it is the middle one to which the world salutes and the solar system dips and that the universe acknowledges.

The earth roars; lightening blazes its fury; a dull shroud of sorrow flings across the afternoon sky.

A keening cry is heard: "*SURELY THIS WAS THE SON OF GOD.*"

A Line. A Mark. The ultimate Mark of a Line.

CHAPTER 5

Too Short, His Road

It is on his eighteenth birthday that he is admitted to the hospital and placed in a bed. The doctor comes in, measures him as he lies, and records on the chart that his height is six feet and four inches.

The pain had come on gradually, and finally, when his legs grew slightly numb, he was taken to the doctor. The doctor found nothing wrong, smiled, and gave Tim some vitamins. He patted his shoulder as he sent him out the door.

In a few days, the increased numbness and pain sent Tim and his mother back to the doctor's office. In front of a retail store, he had fallen flat on his face. Still, the doctor could find nothing wrong. "Mrs. Forrest, I think this may be psychological. However, I will arrange for a neurologist to see him, to make sure there is nothing else. It will take a couple of weeks to get an appointment."

The mother was adamant that they not be put off. "Look, Doctor. Something definitely is wrong. I had to use a wheelchair to bring Tim into the office."

The doctor soothes her, saying, "Okay, Mrs. Forrest. We will put him in the hospital for some tests."

Literally by the hour, his body fails. By the time he is admitted to the hospital, he has taken on a staggering gait. He shuffles across the room, undresses, and climbs into the bed. Those would be his final steps. The pain increases throughout the evening until it is necessary to begin injections of narcotic drugs. He looses control of his bowels, and a nurse inserts a catheter into his bladder.

They take pictures down in the X-ray department, and the doctor comes in with the news. Tim has an enormous growth in his spine. Now both legs are paralyzed. They operate the next day, and the surgeon comes out smiling. "It was a huge tumor, but we got it all out. The frozen section is inconclusive, and we have sent off tissue for further study."

He is okay now, they say, although they will keep him in the intensive care unit for a few days.

Some of our family stay at the hospital day and night during the next few days. There is a small cubicle just outside the ICU, and we wait there for the five minutes each hour that we are permitted to go in. His mother and grandmother spend every night in those chairs.

The permanent section report may take as long as seven days the doctor tells us, but on the third day, he finds the family member who is there: "The radiologist called, and I am afraid I have bad news. Tim has cancer, a kind called Osteogenic Sarcoma. This particular cancer usually strikes young adult males. It is so virulent that if it were in the small toe, the whole leg would have to be amputated." Tim's is in his spine. "We did get out the entire tumor, but it will return as there are invisible cells that will grow again."

The marriage of Daddy and Betty Sue had produced all sons. Mark is older than Tim, Nathan comes next, and David is the youngest. Tim has always been a very sweet boy, quiet and undemanding. Now, in a mysterious way, he begins to glide away from the rest of us. Relentlessly, he moves, daily distancing himself, his life road seen now to be a highly abbreviated one. Too short, his road, it seems to us.

Who is the young boy who lies there on the bed? Who is this fledgling man who returns my gaze? Oh, yes, I know him. His name is Tim. Tim, my younger brother. But who is he? Who is he truly? There must be more than his flawed body would argue. Who is he? What is he? Where will he go?

I deliberate about it all, rehearsing the lines I have been spooned and that I have spooned out myself. The real person is eternal and never will be destroyed, neither by cancer, by accident, nor by old age. I know that, know it well, yet its glaring reality, especially when it is revealed at unexpected and seemingly unfair times, is of distinct and distasteful impact. Tim begins to leave his body, and day by day, it is evident that his failing body really is not Tim. I look into his eyes and try to see him, the real person, but even as I look, I know I see only his house, his shell that is broken and that will not allow repair.

Tim feels better and in a few days is moved from the ICU into a more comfortable and pleasant room. His recovery from the surgery progresses smoothly. The paralysis of his legs continues, albeit with some slight improvement as he can now wiggle a couple of toes. After a week, he is discharged. Doctors say they will begin chemotherapy once he has recovered from the surgery.

Heretofore, he has not been told the full details. One evening, a large group of ministers comes to pray with him, and at one point, when everyone else is out of the room, Tim asks his mother, "Mom, am I going to die?"

Weeping, she admits his grim prognosis and urgently reminds him that when the ministers return to his room, he personally needs to pray for his own salvation. He is a stoic young man, understands his situation, and asks the ministers to come again to his room. Within five minutes, Tim has been enveloped by the love of God, and has received the Holy Ghost.

The doctors have conferred and recommend that Tim be taken to the medical center of the University of California at Los Angeles, whose staff include some of the finest oncologists in the country. When he has been at UCLA for only a short time, the doctors speak frankly: "Mr. Forrest, Mrs. Forrest, chemotherapy would make Tim violently ill, and there is almost no chance that it would help him. The choice is yours, and we will do as you say."

By now, the tumor has regrown, forming a rounded hump on Tim's back. The decision is left to Tim, and he easily makes it. "I want to go home."

When Tim first gets home, there are some good days. His flesh is shrinking though, the calories he takes in going to nourish the monster that feeds on him. He sits in a wheelchair a portion of the day, and then one day is the last for that. The tumor is very large again, and it causes extreme pain as he is moved about. The wheelchair is folded.

"Keep him home as long as you can," the doctor says. "It is most important now to keep him calm."

Stay calm as your body goes away? How? How does one do that? I look at him and wonder.

I stand before the bathroom mirror and look intently into my own eyes. I try to see myself. Who am I? Where? What do I really look like? Who and what is the real me? I frankly struggle with questions and with uncertainty, frustratingly unable to wrap into a tidy package the universal concerns that surely have plagued humankind since antiquity.

One day as I visit, Tim's pain is fierce. He rolls his head back and forth, then for a moment, he looks directly at me, through me, maybe, and I think I catch a glimpse of the true Tim—trapped and frantic inside a rotting body.

His bones become prominent, decubitus areas develop on one of his hips, and the pain increases. The tumor is unbelievably large, making it impossible for him to lie on his back. The home nurse teaches Tim's mother the accepted protocol for needles and narcotics.

Today, nothing will stay on his stomach, and the ambulance comes. The attendants tenderly lift him from the bed, place him on a gurney, and motor him to the hospital. It is not an emergency; sirens do not wail. Only the family wail, a silent cry made of sucked-up grief and sorrow.

There he lies now. One by one, the prescribed narcotics have failed, each replaced by one more potent than before. Several days ago, the doctor said, "It will be any minute now." We pray it is so, and when Tim continues his painful struggle, we ask, "Is it possible he could live this way very long?"

Altering his earlier prediction, the doctor painfully admits, "I am sorry, but conceivably, he could live in this condition for several weeks. I do not think he will, but he is young with a strong heart and clear lungs."

...and then I watch him die.

As the time draws near, the urging comes on me to observe the laying aside of the tent. Although of new canvas, the threads are faulty and lie now on the hospital bed rent and distorted.

I do not long to see the distress or the passing, yet I stand in fascinated looking. He hardly moves, for surely he cannot. Sometimes the nurse comes and gently tends to him. He is a baby...an old man...naked and withered, yet only for eighteen spans has he seen the falling of winter leaves and felt the heat of August on his tender back. Barely has he understood—his eyes still wide—as from earthy depths tender shoots thrust into glorious springtime.

A breath, a long ingathering of air, mouth wide, upper lip reaching for more air. Nostrils wide to gather in the life forces, held long at the apex. Then out again. The last one... no more...then another...then truly no more.

CHAPTER 6

End of the Trail?

Perhaps because I lived in town, I seldom rode horses when I was a child. My only clear memory of such an occasion is a time when two of my cousins and I sat together on the back of a horse with a burlap sack as a saddle. Suddenly, we began to slip. I'm not sure if it was our makeshift saddle that failed, or if one of us caused the commotion that followed, but one by one, we slipped off the rear end of that gray horse. The horse must have been very gentle, for he stood motionless while we three girls scrambled around until we were safely away from his deadly hooves. I certainly had not ridden as an adult; indeed, it is well known among my family and friends that I am quite lacking in athletic skills, and I think it possible that my attempts at such activities continue to be a source of humor to some people.

This day—the end-of-the-trail day—unbelievably, I, Shirley Buxton, nervously sat astride a young mare, high in the Sawtooth Mountains of southern Idaho. The elevation was 8,000 feet.

We stood at the edge of the world. Spread below were verdant valleys, edged by evergreen forests that had expertly climbed the hills and positioned themselves to create breathtaking vistas and indescribable views. Throughout the morning's ascent, our horses had picked their way along the chattering brooks that cut through the countryside. Here and there lay fallen logs, bleached by hot sun and frigid snow. Autumn winds had stripped the leaves from many of the Aspens, although, yet, an occasional one held a glimmering remnant. The locals call the trees "Quakies," a vivid description of the quickening of their small, round leaves. Our party was five. It was led by Everett, whose horse mine had followed closely all day. Often, Everett held my horse's lead rope in consideration of my raw inexperience and probably out of concern for my well-being. Long ago, we had left Little Skeleton Creek Trail

Number Sixty-four, our horses pressing us over unmarked rugged ground as we searched for the deer my armed friends desired. (Only equipped with a Minolta 7000, I had done more "shooting" than the rest had.) Throughout the day, I had been impressed with Everett's kindness, his horsemanship, and his knowledge of the wilderness mountains. Now though, I supposed he had erred.

Everett brought us up short, and at the edge of the world, we paused. Sheer precipice bent the path on which our heaving horses stood. "This looks like the end of the trail, huh Everett?" I quizzed, thinking surely we would turn and find another way down the mountain.

"End of the trail," he parroted in his quiet way. Then, smiling slightly, he turned his horse's head and spoke horrifying words to me. "We will go down right here." With that, he kicked his horse's sides and started straight down the side of the mountain. Bouncing up and down in the saddle, I followed, having no option: my horse's lead rope was in Everett's wide hand. Jerry was behind, bringing up the rear horse. As we talked later, he agreed that the grade was thirty to forty percent. It was unbelievable.

Terror raced through me, digging into my lungs and jerking hoarse gasps from my throat. I simply could not believe it. How could I be here? Me—a fifty year old woman, fairly sedentary, who had never ridden before. Was I actually on this lathered animal high in the Sawtooths ready to plunge to the valley?

It had been an outstanding trip to this point. Jerry and I and our friends, Berl and Lavelta Stevenson, had been together for three weeks combining vacation time with business. We traveled in nearly identical ancient Travco motorhomes that we had restored. We had journeyed from southern California to Salt Lake where we attended a church conference at the Salt Palace. We parked our rigs at the local KOA.

At the conclusion of the conference, we spent a few days exploring antique stores in the area. Wednesday afternoon, we wheeled along Utah's roadway 150, the young proprietor of Salt Lake's Brass Ring Antiques having suggested that we must not fail to drive the seventy-eight miles that stretched from Kamas, Utah into Evanston, Wyoming. The advice was excellent, revealing scenery that all four of us, fairly well traveled persons, agreed to be some of the most spectacular we had ever seen. We picked up material at the Kamas ranger station that marked fifty-two areas of interest within those seventy-eight miles. It was mid afternoon when we drove into Taylor's Fork Campground. We pulled past its designated parking sites into a wide meadow cut gently by a meandering stream, and there we set camp for the night. There was no one else in the campground. The Wasatch Mountains circled our valley: in the distance, they towered brilliantly into an unclouded sky. The Stevensons had a Lab pup with them—Jacque was his name—and after they loosed him from his carrier, Jerry and I took him for a romp through the woods. He tore through the trees, a frisky golden flash, rustling through leaves and fallen branches as he retrieved the sticks we threw. The trail was a pad of Aspen leaves, an Oriental rug of yellow and rust and brown. We dragged a log back to camp and threw it into a stone fire ring that someone had fashioned. We ate a simple dinner. The guys listened to a World Series ball game, and we turned in early. The night was soot; there was no moon. In my bed, as I ambled through that semi-conscious state immediately before sleep, I faintly heard gentle water breaking over stone.

Thursday morning, I followed my early morning motorhome ritual. Shortly after dawn, I jumped from bed, dashed four steps to turn up the thermostat, lighted the flame under the waiting coffeepot, then dived back under the snug covers. I dozed until the aroma of perking coffee tugged me out again. After Jerry and I had our first cup of coffee, we explored the other end of the empty campground. It had been very cold during the night, and a heavy frost covered the land. Sunbeams spotlighted the frost particles, transforming the land into a veritable fairy world. Diamonds had sprung up. I crouched near a log to photograph the jewels, but it was a fleeting show, for in minutes, the heat had dissolved them, and they dripped deep into the crevice of the log.

The entire day had been as splendid as its beginning. We continued our trek over highway 150, judging it as magnificent as the portion we saw the day before. We wore heavy jackets and stopped often to tramp over enticing trails, and to perch on gray stone that overlooked lakes and streams. As we looked and walked, we ate and drank—drank from deep cups of coffee and munched on tasty oatmeal cookies. We babbled on our CBs. The highway wound ever upward, then snow lay beside the roadway and the tree branches were shrouds of white. Occasionally, yellow leaves flared. Finally, we reached the pass—just over 10,000 feet the sign said. Hayden Peak loomed in the distance, at an elevation of 12,000 feet. A canyon gaped before us showing a majestic mountain that rose on the far side, its peak swallowed in fog. We stopped to absorb the splendor and to snap pictures as we tried to capture the spirit of this magnificent territory.

Originally, it was our plan to head home at this point and to part company with the Stevensons, who would travel alone to Idaho. Instead, through a series of timely circumstances, we found ourselves tailing after our friends and becoming involved with the hunting trip. In Twin Falls, we spent a day and a half restocking our rig and buying warmer clothing. The men took Jerry to the sports store, and he bought a hunting license.

Everett led us out of Twin Falls on Monday evening, heading for the south fork of the Boise River. Our friends

Elaine and Allen Picklesimer, residents of Twin Falls and the originators of the annual expedition, joined the caravan with a truck and a fifth-wheel vehicle. Everett's wife, Stella, rode with him in the camper truck that towed a horse trailer with five quarter horses inside. The Stevensons and Buxtons completed the entourage of assorted vehicles, sturdy mountain horses, and eight mighty hunters! The trek was strenuous, elevating us several thousand feet, then turning us down a deep canyon by a winding road that seemed to go on forever. The last nineteen miles were a dirt and gravel road of such roughness that we were afraid our motorhome would shake apart. It was impossible to carry on a decent conversation, as we had to shout if we wanted to speak to each other. When we arrived, we found that the severe shaking had turned on the shower, and all our water had run into the bathtub. We set camp in the dark, and at about eleven o'clock, we wearily tumbled into bed.

We awoke to grandeur. Our camp sat on the banks of the Boise River. It flowed shallow and swift and was so clear that I could see its rocky bottom from one side to the other. From the far bank rose a steep forest of fragrant pines with wide meadows punctuated here and there by granite formations. Blazing Aspens painted the last strokes of perfection.

Tuesday was a day set to scout around as the hunters prepared for Wednesday when they would match wits with the deer in the area. My intent had not been to hunt, or even to ride a horse during this campout, so to this day, I am not sure how the rest of this story unfolded. Somehow, on that particular Tuesday, I found myself mounted on a horse, (although it was a feat just to get myself into the saddle), and I had joined the scouting party! I dubbed my unnamed horse "California," and I did all right, I suppose, for by Tuesday evening, I had made the commitment to join the other hunters on Wednesday for the opening day of deer hunting. Unbelievable. At first light on Wednesday morning, we were on the trail, ascending steadily. Now, near day's end, we were ready to return to camp.

It seemed we were going straight down, but actually, Everett led us back and forth over the mountain face, a trailing method designed to minimize the steep descent. The terrain was rough and unsteady. Rock and shale tumbled freely, disturbed by the pawing of those massive horses. I had been effusive all day, chattering freely and raving about the beauty of the wilderness area. "Wish my kids could see me now," I spoke earlier in the day as I sat high in the saddle. Now, I was terrified, a lump who sat heavy atop my horse. My hands held onto whatever they could find, and my short legs jerked in and out of the stirrups.

We were three quarters of the way down the mountainside when Everett's horse skidded and began edging sideways, skittering into an out-of-control dance. Then California swung an arc around him, and wildly, I began bouncing up and down, unable at all to keep my feet in the stirrups. I yelled, "I'm coming off!" For a minute, I thought I could recover. Then I was off and over my horse's head. I was a ball rolling on the ground, and now, somehow, my terror was gone, and I was all practicality. I thought of the hooves of my horse and prayed, "Please, stand still, California."

When I stopped rolling, a lead ceiling of silence had lowered and was as thick and ominous as funeral air. No one spoke. My trail mates were stunned mutes, and I raised myself to grin at them so they could breathe again. Someone gathered the boots that had pitched from my feet, and they examined me with cautious eyes. Everett was anxious for my well-being and generous with apology for his part in the fiasco. Miraculously, I was not at all hurt. We were still an hour out of camp, and I definitely did not feel the need for any more horseback riding, but neither was I prepared to walk out of the forest, so after resting, again I mounted California. I sat squarely in her saddle, and by nightfall, we were in camp.

We were still in bed the next morning when Jerry asked me to reach up and turn on the light. As I began to move, the pain that blasted throughout every tortured part of my being distinctly revealed my fifty-year-old body to have unmistakable memories of its first hunting trip.

Life is a journey, a twisting and bending adventure. Only those who take the challenge will ride to the apex. End of the trail? Hardly. Before the trip was over, I had bought myself a red cowgirl hat.

CHAPTER 7
The Runaway Bus

The week before, a storm had moved down the coast, pounding several inches of rain into the hardened earth of southern California. It smattered a farewell of hail, then moved into the mountain ranges that surround the Los Angeles basin, and proceeded into the San Bernardino Mountains. Splendid snow blanketed the resort areas before the storm moved out. It was welcome weather, for the drought had been devastating, one of costly agricultural losses and one that had forced the closure of many ski runs. It was a tremendous storm; the drought, at least for the time, was ended.

Now the weather was mid-winter bright and of that rarified, smog-less type that serves to make southern California the envy of the rest of the country. Monday, February 16, was the last of the five-day Presidents' Birthdays holiday. Thousands of southern Californians took to the mountains.

Kenneth Jackson was the youth leader of a church in Garden Grove, and he and his wife chose this holiday to take a group of nineteen youngsters to an area near Big Bear Lake for a day of snow play. The bus was a 54-passenger Chevy, and they had an uneventful two-hour trip over the freeway system and up Highway 330. They parked in a service station lot.

The youngsters were excited and chattered with anticipation. They unloaded the equipment, grabbed their snacks, and raced up and down the slopes all day. They had a wonderful time, some hardly pausing to eat. In mid-afternoon, exhausted, but aglow with the exhilaration of the day, they clambered aboard the bus. As Kenneth Jackson checked the bus before boarding, he was dismayed to see that one of the tires was flat. While the young people settled themselves, he asked the station attendant to help with the tire. The mechanic was unable to repair it but pumped it up, and then directed him to another station down the highway. They too, were unable to repair the tire. He boarded the bus and cautiously drove to a nearby tire center for a replacement.

Finally, the split-rim tire was changed. Freezing ice crunched under his feet, and the afternoon shadows lengthened as Kenneth walked toward the bus for the trip down the mountain. "Is everybody situated?" He faced the twenty people. "We're ready to head home."

At home, the media were telling of traffic alerts and warning of snarls and tangles on all mountain highways. At one point earlier in the day, on nearby Mt. Baldy, Shinn Road had been closed to all uphill traffic. Presses were busy clacking out the words of U. S. Forest Service dispatcher, Bob Underwood: "You could walk from Foothill Blvd. to Mt. Baldy on top of them [cars]." A California Highway Patrol spokesman was reporting that the normal one-hour trip from Big Bear Lake to San Bernardino was taking four to five hours and that traffic was traveling at about one mile an hour.

The radio warned of these traffic problems, but on the bus, they had no radio, and they heard no reports. Kenneth Jackson checked the group for the final time. "Is everybody ready?" He sat down in his seat, started the engine, and after looking in his mirrors, joined the other traffic on the highway.

The traffic *was* fierce. Everyone seemed to be heading home and hoping to get out of the mountains before dark fell. The bus traveled for an hour and a half in stop-and-go fashion: one mile an hour, now two, then one again. The traffic was lined, bumper to bumper. At one time, when they slowed to a mere crawl, some of the youngsters climbed off the bus and ran forward to see if there could have been an accident. "Nothing," they said as they climbed back into the bus. "Just a lot of traffic. Boy, is it cold out there."

The traffic moved slightly, stopped, then crept forward, stopped, slowed, then picked up again. The day grew dark: Kenneth switched on the headlights. Streaming behind them were hundreds of cars, their headlights glaring now; ahead were hundreds more. A line of red taillights streaked down the mountain. The young people talked loudly and sang, then fell quiet as fatigue lulled some of them to sleep. Toward the front of the bus, the adults talked softly.

"Hey, Brother Jackson, I smell the brakes."

Kenneth checked the brake pedal, tapping gently. "They seem fine. Actually, I have used them relatively little. I have been gearing down so the brakes won't get hot. Probably, you are smelling exhaust fumes."

"Okay, Brother Jackson."

He continued to use the gears as much as he could to restrain the bus. Now the descent steepened. Cars cleared out a bit, and for a while, there was space in front of the bus. He shifted and accelerated slightly to stay apace, then the gap closed again. He downshifted to slow the bus, but with the steeper incline and the momentum he had gained, the gears alone would no longer hold the bus. *I must brake now,* he thought. He raised his right leg, placed his foot on the brake pedal, and pushed downward. The pedal hit the floor with a sound thump. He pushed again. Nothing! Rapidly now, the bus gained speed. Frantically, he looked at the crowded highway. He fairly jammed the pedal. Nothing. *I don't have any brakes,* he thought. *Oh, God, the brakes are out on this bus.*

He turned his head slightly so that all could hear him. In a tense voice, but with calm deliberation, he shouted the warning, "Pray everyone. Please pray. The brakes are out on the bus."

For a moment, there was stunned, flat silence, then an explosion of hysterical screaming. As though by signal, hands shot into the air, and divine intervention was invoked. "Help us, God. Help us!"

Kenneth fought for control of the bus. *Stay calm,* he ordered himself. *My God, I'm responsible for these lives. Help me, God; please help me. My God, what can I do?*

The bus continued to gain speed. Now it was up to 30 miles an hour, and he had closed the gap ahead of him. The taillights of the car ahead were too close: he was about to ram that car. "Hold on, everybody. I've got to move over." He whipped the bus out of the line and into the oncoming lane. Mercifully, there were no cars approaching, and now he had no choice except to stay in that lane. The other lane, on his right now, was a thick, steady stream of cars, and he could not slow down enough to pull back in. The car passengers stared aghast as the bus streaked by.

Many of the youngsters were at the windows now screaming. "Move over, move over, please move over." Kathy leaned over from her seat near the front and pushed desperately on the horn.

"Keep blowing it, Kathy. Don't stop." Kenneth Jackson threw the terse command to his daughter.

The bus roared on, going ever faster as it bolted down the mountain. *I have to do something. I absolutely must. Please help me, God.* Shaking violently, Kenneth Jackson lifted his right hand from the steering wheel and placed it on the gearshift. He pulled desperately, trying to force the transmission into a lower gear. He groaned as he felt a violent vibration. The synchros refused to mesh, but instead gave out a loud grinding noise. The transmission was still in second gear as he deliberately placed his hand on the ignition key, turned it, and killed the motor. Maybe the dead engine would form enough compression to slow the out-of- control bus. No. No change. No slowing. The engine was silent now as the bus thundered on. Tires screamed on the pavement below.

It probably is best that I ram this bus into the side of one of these mountains. I can't keep this up. We're going faster every second, and any time now, there is bound to come a car in this lane. He glanced to his left. A sheer cliff dropped 1000 feet into a gaping canyon, and to the right was the endless stream of cars. *No way. I cannot do that. I can't ram this bus. We're going too fast It would kill us all. Please help me, God. Please help us.*

Richard Bruckner stood up and walked to the front of the bus. *There's no way we are going to make it. All of us will be killed,* he thought. *I'm getting out of here.* He grabbed the handle, opened the front door, and jumped out. Only two people on the bus saw him. They were speechless with fear and could not tell anyone.

Suddenly, headlights loomed in Kenneth Jackson's eyes. A car was coming up the hill. *Oh God.* His heart was a hammer in his chest. He jerked his head around and frantically looked to the right. A tiny opening in the line. He whipped over. The car coming up flashed by on their left. Then frantically, he jerked the bus from the line and back into the oncoming lane. He was too close to the truck ahead of them, and as they veered past, the bus ripped off the truck's side mirror. "Pray, people, pray." *Oh God, please help us. What are we going to do?*

....40 miles an hour...50 ...the speed gathered.

In the seats behind Kenneth Jackson, sheer terror dominated and pandemonium filled the bus. The air reverberated with screamed prayers, and with pleas for Godly mercy and for His intervention. The young minds were inundated with thoughts that ran the gamut from surrender to the will of God to visions of burning in hell.

All that playing church...the rebellion, the listening
to foul music. I'm going to hell. I really am. No, I'm not.
God is merciful. Forgive me, God.

Well, this is it. Why can't I pray? I always thought I'd have time to repent, but now I can't even pray.

Kim rose from her seat and with outstretched hands, walked to Rebecca. Her fingers were curled grotesquely from fear. "Help me, Becky, help me!"

Frantically, Rebecca motioned to her friend. "Sit down and shut up, Kim." Kim would have no memory of it.

Well, this is it, God. I'm coming home. I feel a sort of peace and acceptance of it.

This can't be real; it just can't be.

Those cliffs on the side! Oh, God, we're going over.

Colleen reached for the seat ahead of her, her arms outstretched and stiffened. Then she remembered someone saying that if she should ever be involved in a wreck, she should try to relax. She loosened her grip, closed her eyes, and slumped down into the seat.

Screaming. I think I'm screaming. Jesus!

God, get me out of this, and I will serve you forever.

The Lord is my shepherd, I shall not want.

Nicky had seen Richard Bruckner when he jumped from the bus. Nicky grabbed his brother, Tony, pushed him to the floor, and sat on top of him. "Stay in the floor, Tony. Stay down."

Forgive me, God. Help us. Please help us.

I feel stunned and unable to move.

Suddenly, Vicky Bruckner whirled around in her seat. "Where's Richard? Where's my husband?"

Nicky looked into her unbelieving eyes and said, "He jumped out. He jumped out of the bus back there."

"He what?" Vicky screamed. "Richard. Oh God, where is Richard?"

The bus roared on. Kenneth Jackson continued his fight at the wheel. Another car came up the hill, then another. He was frantic, his desperate eyes searching for a place to pull into the right lane. There was none. Nearly senseless with fear, he gripped the wheel and stayed his position. At the last minute, the startled driver of each car pulled as far as possible to the right, and the bus screamed by. Unrelenting, the narrow mountain road twisted beside deep canyons and across constricted bridges. Protective railings flashed by. The curves were of such degree that once the bus tilted until it was riding on two wheels. Another sharp curve. The ground seemed level with the side windows.

...60 miles an hour...70...The road yet descended. Purses and food and clothing were flying through the bus. The people were thrown back and forth and into the seats ahead and were slammed into the side walls. Debris littered the floors. Their eyes were glazed as they screamed or sat dumb.

Suddenly, the bus slowed. *We're slowing down.* Kenneth Jackson searched outside with his eyes. *It appears that we still are going down, but it feels as though we are going up.* It was definite now. The speed of the bus was decreasing. Kenneth saw a space in the right hand lane, and he pulled into it. *Ram the mountain. Ram it now.* He decided that was the thing to do. He steeled himself, turned the wheel, and watched as the mountain rushed at the bus. *Help, God. Help me. This seems the only thing to do. Oh God, I hope this is right.*

It is impossible to explain what happened next, except to say that on occasion, without a doubt, there is supernatural intervention in the pitiful lives of men. Kenneth Jackson was emotionally drained and physically exhausted as he deliberately turned the bus and its twenty-one passengers into the side of the mountain. Seconds before impact, he distinctly and clearly saw a giant hand reach downward. Ugly scars were visible as the hand reached out and pushed back the bus. Slam! Then stop. Stop. They had stopped. Kenneth Jackson, nearly insensible, slumped deep in his seat.

When Rebecca felt the dull thud of impact, she thought they had gone over a cliff, and she passed out.

A van roared up. "We have one of your men here." Vicky ran screaming to Richard. When he jumped, he landed in the direct line of traffic. He heard cars screeching and swerving to miss him. Then someone stopped and lifted Richard safely from the street.

An ambulance came quickly, taking Rebecca and Richard to a hospital in San Bernardino. Rebecca was unhurt and easily regained consciousness. She watched as Richard's wounds were stitched. He held his arms straight up in the air, repeating often: "Whatever you want me to do God, I surely will do it." His clothes were in shreds, the metal on his shoes was filed off, but he suffered no broken bones, nor any other serious injuries.

Back at the bus, both Sheila and Colleen went into shock and were taken to an area hospital where they were treated and released. Along with others, Tammy walked around the bus, laughing and crying and praying. An officer walked by, patted her on the shoulder, and said soothingly, "It's okay, honey. You're all right now."

A large number of people stopped to commend Kenneth Jackson for the way he handled the bus. Many of them offered their services. Three people left their names. "Free feel to call on us if you need any corroboration that this indeed was a miracle." (These names are on file at Forrest Press.)

"I never believed in God until I saw this today," one young man said as he pushed his way through the crowd.

The dreadful out-of-control bus ride had ranged in speed from 20 miles an hour to 78 miles an hour. They had navigated twelve sharp curves and passed by three 1000 feet drop-offs as well as numerous others of less depth. They crossed two bridges, passed approximately 300 cars, and met three head on. All this was without serious injury to anyone.

It surely was an undisputed miracle. But why was such a thing done at this particular moment? If God can supernaturally stop a bus, why did He allow the crisis in the beginning? As long as we live, no doubt, we will grapple for absolute answers to such questions. Some reasons, though, are obvious. Such an experience results in a keen spiritual awareness and a renewing of dedication, both to God and to man. Every person who rode the bus that day must certainly acknowledge that absolute truth. Living through such a traumatic, but certainly victorious experience, causes us to acknowledge the weakness and frailty of man. Anew, and in unsullied form, we place God at the very center of our lives.

It seems right to offer thanks.

CHAPTER 8
The Way of Holiness

Within the heart of every child of God resonates a desire for holiness and purity. Inherent in our spirit is the urge to take on genuine attributes of godliness and righteousness, to walk closer to Jesus every day, and to refine our attitudes and actions until His very nature becomes our own. Not only do we crave these qualities for ourselves, but because of spiritual understanding, we also covet this essence for our family and for our friends. It has become clear to us that the victorious life comes only through the pursuit of righteousness and holiness. I use the word pursuit advisedly, acknowledging that within ourselves we cannot take on these attributes, but knowing too that the harder we pursue Jesus, the more of His nature we will assume. God did say in Leviticus 20:7, "*...Be ye holy....*" It is fair to believe that since God Himself issued that commandment, it *is* possible for a human being to be holy. Be warned, however, that the principles and practice of holiness stand in direct contrast to the decadence and corruption that define the world. Man has sunk to such a state of immorality and has become so polluted that what once was considered perverted now gleamingly has been labeled normal and upright. At every turn, satan and his followers endeavor to thrust their demonic illusions upon us, and those of a holiness bent are often marked as prejudiced and judgmental and as having the attitude of a Pharisee.

Let me go further and say that it is not only the people of God who long for holy and righteous living. Because of His unsearchable love, God knocks at the heart of every man and points to the Way of Holiness. Tired of sin and debauchery, many respond and without reserve open themselves to the ways of God and fully obey the New Testament plan of salvation. "*Now when they heard this,* [a sermon by Peter] *they were pricked in their heart, and said unto Peter and to the rest of the apostles, Men and brethren, what shall we do?*

Then Peter said unto them, Repent, and be baptized every one of you in the name of Jesus Christ for the remission of sins, and ye shall receive the gift of the Holy Ghost" (Acts 2:37-38).

"In South America there is a tree, so travelers say, the leaf of which starving men will chew, because it gives them the most enjoyable sensations of having been fed. Through its influences, all desire for food departs, and a starving person is thus saved from the painful gnawing of hunger. Pain is taken away, but death is not defeated. The leaf contains a drug, but no nourishment. It satisfies a man's craving, but it does not satisfy his need, for in one respect it is a counterfeit of food; it deceives the dying man by assuring him that he has had food, whereas he is dying for lack of it.

This is exactly the danger which attends a form of godliness. It meets and satisfies the inner craving of our religious natures, and yet it is a spiritual drug plunging us into death when we think we have found life. It satisfies our craving, but it does not provide for our need. It fills, but it does not feed."[9]

Let the first part of this chapter resolutely point to that which goes far beyond mere form and appearance. It is called the Way of Holiness, and what a splendid, magnificent road it is. Listen to Isaiah's description in chapter 35 verses 8 and 9: *"And an highway shall be there, and a way, and it shall be called The way of holiness; the unclean shall not pass over it; but it shall be for those; the wayfaring men, though fools, shall not err therein.*

No lion shall be there, nor any ravenous beast shall go up thereon, it shall not be found there; but the redeemed shall walk there:"

HOLINESS SKETCHED

Think about it. It is a high way, not a low way. It is a desirable place, not a dreaded one. It is not a certain look, dull drab clothes, or a pious face, low and cast down. The distinctive look of a Christian does not make us holy, nor does the flawless understanding of the plan of salvation. Holiness is not judgment or a list of dos and don'ts. Rather, holiness is fully embracing the Word of God and looks beyond fashionable teachings and the traditions of men. Holiness calls for a willingness to listen and truly to hear. It is a resplendent place, lustrous and brilliant with unearthly light. There is no need to dig in our heels and refuse to go, as though someone is trying to convince us of something or take us where we do not want to be. The Highway of Holiness conveys joyful peace and a happy contentment. A calm mind and holy security inhabit its lanes. C. S. Lewis has well said, "How little people know who think that holiness is dull. When one meets the real thing, it is irresistible…"[10]

Verse 4 of the previously referred to chapter (Isaiah 35) relates that God Himself walks on the highway. It must be high and holy, for He is there. Only God and the redeemed traverse that way, for the unclean cannot come. It is a virtuous, preferred place, a bright and shining course. Jeremiah 6:16 calls it a good way.

Keil and Delitzsch comment: "Not only unclean persons from among the heathen, but even unclean persons belonging to Israel itself, will never pass along that holy road, none but the church purified and sanctified through suffering and those connected with it. To them and them alone, does this road belong, which Jehovah has made and secured and which so readily strikes the eye, …whilst it lies too high, that no beast of prey, however powerful could possibly leap up to it: not one is ever encountered by the pilgrim there."

Holiness is a posture toward God, an approach of submission that gives Him absolute control of our lives. More than all else, holiness is an attitude. A wonderful story of an accomplished musician and a small child illustrates this.

"Ignace Jan Paderewski, the famous Polish pianist and statesman, was once scheduled to perform at a great concert hall in America. It was a black-tie affair—a high-society extravaganza.

Present in the audience that evening was a woman who had brought her nine-year-old son, hoping that he would be encouraged to practice the piano if he could just hear the great Paderewski at the keyboard. Weary of waiting for the concert to begin—and being there against his wishes anyway—the lad squirmed restlessly in his seat. Then, as his mother turned to talk with friends, the boy slipped out of his seat and down the aisle, strangely drawn by the ebony concert grand sitting majestic and alone at the center of the huge stage. He sat down on the tufted leather stool, placed his small hands on the black and white keys, and began to play "Chop Sticks."

Suddenly the crowd hushed, and hundreds of frowning faces turned in his direction. Irritated and embarrassed, some began to shout: "Hey, get that boy away from there!" "Where's his mother?" "Somebody stop him!"

Backstage, Paderewski heard the uproar and the sound of the simple tune. When he saw what was happening, he hurried onto the stage. Without a word to the audience, he walked up behind the lad, reached his arms around either side of him, and began to improvise a countermelody. As the two made music together, the master pianist kept whispering in the boy's ear: "Keep going. Don't quit, son. Keep on playing...don't stop...don't quit."[11]

Oh that we could submit as completely as did that young child. May we recognize God when He comes and when

He places His hands over ours. Give us the sense to hear His whispers and the trust to leave our hands motionless beneath His.

The remarkable thing about the Way of Holiness is that God individually chooses us who walk there. Think about it. God's words concerning separation are not hard sayings at all but reveal an exceptional thought: God wants us to be clean, pure, and holy and to live a separated, dedicated life because *He wants us for Himself.*

II Corinthians 6:17: "*Wherefore come out from among them, and be ye separate, saith the Lord, and touch not the unclean thing; and I will receive you,*"

Ephesians 1:4 says, "*According as he hath chosen us in him before the foundation of the world, that we should be holy and without blame before him in love:*"

Psalm 4:3 says, "*But know that the LORD hath set apart him that is godly for himself:...*"

What tremendous insight David reveals in that scripture, an understanding that we often overlook. Not only do we need God and desire Him, but He longs for us, and in one sense of the word, He needs us. He loves us, knows who we are, loves us anyway, and has fashioned a unique place for us. We walk with Him and commune with Him along the Way of Holiness. Come, my beloved, Jesus says. Come. Walk here with me; fellowship with me. Let us talk together.

Psalm 42:1 and 2: "*As the hart panteth after the water brooks, so panteth my soul after thee, O God. My soul thirsteth for God, for the living God: ...*"

In precious and singular fashion, God is concerned with us as we walk this way. He has not asked that, alone, we feel our way down a hard and narrow place. This is a glorious place, and God Himself is beside us, encouraging and supporting us because we have responded to His invitation to walk the Highway of Holiness.

The apostle Paul, writing to the early church, says, "*And the very God of peace sanctify you wholly...*" (I Thessalonians 5:23).

I love that. It is God who sanctifies me and who sanctifies you. He cares enough to purify us and to see that we develop into a holy people. It is not our mother who sanctifies us, not our dad, not the person who introduced us to Jesus, not our best friend, not even the preacher. God will. He wants us to be holy, and once any of us moves in that direction, God steps right out and meets us—meets us far more than half way. When God sees a person who is striving for holiness, I believe He smiles and moves—moves in and gets right down into the middle of that life. (I believe it is impossible to talk about God and say it exactly right. Consider the words—*God moves.* How can God move when He occupies all space? I will leave those issues to you who are smarter than I!)

I urge you to consider these scriptures carefully, to ponder them, and to inculcate them into your thinking. They reveal the extreme interest God takes in us, not just us, as in us The Church, but us, as in me, you, each of us as individuals.

"*But I am poor and needy; yet the Lord thinketh upon me...*" (Psalm 40:17). Can we grasp that? He thinks on *us*, on *you* and *me.* He considers me—when I struggle to pay my bills, when I may lose my house, when I have made foolish moves and put myself in a terrible bind, when the utilities may be cut off, and when Visa cancels my charge card. God sees it and thinks about it; He thinks on me. When I lack the gas to run errands, when I have no money to buy shoes for the children, God knows about it—and He does care. He is involved with me, for we are walking together on the Highway of Holiness.

"*...no good thing will he withhold from them that walk uprightly*" (Psalm 84:11).

The Word of God is absolute, and it is a truth that He will withhold nothing good from us. Sometimes, we may want something to happen and may even consider it good for us, but God may be of another mind. Such things may work to our detriment, perhaps even hindering our walk with Him. But if it is good for us, in His perfect way and time, He will allow us to have that.

"*Being confident of this very thing, that he which hath begun a good work in you will perform it...* (Philippians 1:6).

Ever sense that you started well but that you are not progressing as you should? Do you feel stymied as though a roadblock threatens your way? Are you perplexed and bewildered, a lack of progress annoying and mystifying you? We all have been there; we all have stood at such spot and gazed at our frustrated feet. Although it appears simplistic, I declare the solution quite simple: it lies in the continued walk along the Way of Holiness. That's it. Just keep walking, keep trudging, keep plodding, and keep tramping. Stay your eyes on the leader. I promise you, God will not begin developing us only to forsake us. It just will not happen. It may feel that way, but that is not the case. He walks beside us, and He will finish the work He has begun in us. There may come times when your walk shifts and seems treacherous and when satan points his vile finger at your failures and lack of progress. When that happens, speak the Word of God to him. I recommend the delightful words of Jacob as he dealt with his father-in-law, Laban. They are found in verse 33 of Genesis 30: "*So shall my righteousness answer for me.*"

Isn't that the greatest thing! There is no need to speak up or to defend myself, no call to explain things or to make excuses—none of it. My righteousness answers for me. I am quite aware that if I were acting alone, my righteousness surely would be lacking and inadequate. The great prophet,

Isaiah, speaks to this in chapter 64 verse 6. "*But we are all as an unclean thing, and all our righteousnesses are as filthy rags; and we all do fade as a leaf; and our iniquities, like the wind, have taken us away.*" Nevertheless, it is remarkable that when we have taken on a godly nature, His righteousness is imputed to us; subsequently, His righteousness answers for us. Look at Genesis 15:6 "*And he* [Abraham] *believed in the Lord; and he counted it to him for righteousness.*"

It is not strange to think that once we are born again, we begin to take on a holy nature, for at that time, our disposition radically changes. It is natural for us to be walking the holy way. Holiness has become our nature, and the child of God will find it uncomfortable to rest anywhere except in holiness. In a sermon he once preached, Pastor Carlton Watkins made a profound statement: "Once you get to Calvary, there is no other way to go except toward holiness."[12]

J. L. Hall, the editor of the *Pentecostal Herald*, writes, "While we could not approach God because of our unholiness, His love built a bridge with the cross of Calvary, and provided the path for us to regain the holiness we lost in the Fall."[13]

HOLINESS MANIFEST

Given that this discussion of holiness covers only one chapter in this book, it surely is understood to be a limited and cursory look at the subject; undoubtedly, you comprehend that in no way can its extent and limits be covered in such abbreviated text. Indeed, should we take an entire book, or write accounts to fill every library on the globe, the exposé would be frail, and the subject would in no way be exhausted nor fully delineated. I declare the telling of God's holiness as humanly impossible. For when we talk of holiness, we speak of the nature of God and His attributes, His very being. For that is God—He *is* Holiness. Given then these limitations, we speak only of one aspect of holiness, that of attitude.

Someone has said, "Attitude is not the main thing; it is the only thing." Once we accept any philosophy, its precepts and tentacles must reach into every part of our lives. It flags our thinking and determines our bearing. The one who acclaims virtue and holiness his standard is a fixed star in the midnight sky. Others turn in that direction, for such principles distinguish the attitude of the Holiness Walker, and his responses are noted and respected.

Micah 6:8 "*He hath shewed thee, O man, what is good; and what doth the LORD require of thee, but to do justly, and to love mercy, and to walk humbly with thy God?*"

What powerful, directive scripture. You may wish to take your Bible and read verses 6 and 7 of that same chapter of Micah. Wanting to approach God in the right way, the people ask the question: does the LORD need the sacrifices of thousands of rams, or does He need ten thousands of rivers of oil? Is that what He wants from me? Is that what I must do to please God? Perhaps He wants my firstborn as sacrifice for my sin or another burnt offering. Firmly, the prophet resounds. No, that is not what God wants. His requirements are simple and clearly defined: do justly, love mercy, and walk humbly.

The Holiness Walk demands that the credit for any accomplishments goes to God, an understanding that nothing can be done without Him. It is through Him that we even move and have our being. Our very breath and our thought processes directly flow from Him.

"Mr. [Rev. D. L.] Moody, when holding meetings at St. Louis at one time, was approached after the service by one of his ushers who told him there was a group of the most influential men and women of the city who wished to be introduced to him. This was very flattering attention, surely. Mr. Moody had just delivered one of his most powerful and effective sermons, and was busy here and there with the inquirers, while this company of distinguished people waited to meet the great evangelist. When Mr. Moody had finished all that the Lord had given him to do, he quietly, and unobserved, slipped out of the rear door and went to his room. Later, in explaining his apparent discourtesy, he said that he feared to tarry for the word of adulation and flattery; he must get back to his room and report first to his Lord who had sent him forth."[14]

Some people are brighter and more talented than I am, and their accomplishments more impressive than mine are, precluding me from being in their league as far as ability and achievement are concerned. The Holiness Walk calls for me to honor these people and forbids a jealous, contentious, competitive spirit. At times, all of us accomplish more than at other times; this often due to the normal ebb and flow of life. True holiness calls for a consistent walk—whether blessed with progress and fortune or with situations that prove difficult and challenging, when success seems nowhere around.

It was the year 1978; my husband and I were completely immersed in the work of God and were having some of the best years of our lives. One night Jerry had an unusual dream. At the time of the dream, Jerry was the pastor of Calvary Apostolic Chapel in Garden Grove, CA. and his dream concerned his friend, Rev. Murray Layne, who was the pastor of the United Pentecostal Church in Rialto, CA. The gist of the dream was that Rev. Layne had resigned from his pastorate and was moving to another city.

We are not a family given to direction by dreams, but the dream affected Jerry so much that he mentioned it to me two or three times, and I could tell that he was deeply moved by it. The dream stayed with Jerry for several days, so that although he felt awkward doing so, he finally called Rev. Layne and told him of the dream. There was silence on the telephone line when Jerry finished speaking; then Rev. Layne said, "You're teasing me, aren't you?" Only a few days before, he had resigned his church and already had been chosen as pastor in Mesquite, TX. Naturally thinking Jerry had heard of this development when he told him the dream, he believed Jerry was joking with him.

It was not a joke though, and both of us were stunned to the core as Jerry hung up the telephone and told me of this startling development. We sincerely prayed that we would understand the will of God. Did he want us to leave Garden Grove and go to Rialto? The next day, Jerry decided to travel to Rialto. This was only an hour away, and he could talk at length with Rev. Layne. On the way, he stopped in to see his godly brother, Herbert, who lived in Ontario. Jerry walked into Herb's family room and began telling of the striking developments of the past few days. Herb lifted his hand and said, "Don't tell me. Let me tell you."

Shocked at this, Jerry stood still and listened to the rest of his brother's astounding words. "Murray Layne is leaving Rialto, and you will be the new pastor." God had revealed this to Herb as he prayed that morning.

Indeed, Jerry did assume the pastorate of New Life Center in Rialto, and we were there for almost nineteen years. Although they were not perfect years, they were good years, and looking back, I can think of a few things we accomplished. (I say *we accomplished,* because when we married, we became one flesh, and I like to team with Jerry when it is time to take credit for something well done. Negative stories? A different tune!) I derive joy from thinking on the highly unusual way that God directed us to Rialto and the wonderful days we spent there. I see the magnificent auditorium that was finished under Jerry's leadership, the fellowship hall and the two office additions that were built. There also, Jerry founded a Christian school that will celebrate its 20th year in September of 2003. More than that, I think of the faithful and godly people whose lives we touched during that time. At this moment, I can think of eight men who were called into the ministry during those years. Six of them became pastors, and today, all of them are involved in the work of God. Unique among these men was the late Rev. Don Morrison, who at the age of thirty-seven was stricken with a fatal brain tumor. Always tremendously faithful, at the time of his death, he was in the process of planting a church in Arvada, Colorado. I pay tribute to him today.

I recall when the person who held the mortgage on our church property walked into my husband's office, laid papers on the desk, and said, "The church is paid for. The rest of the debt is forgiven. You owe nothing." Thus when we left Rialto, there sat eight beautiful acres and two impressive buildings, totally debt free to be turned over to the new pastor.

Stunning words are found in I Corinthians 10:24: "*Let no man seek his own, but every man another's wealth*."

Consider carefully that the Way of Holiness asks that a man not be ambitious for himself, rather that he consider the needs and feelings of others. This attitude is in direct contrast to the carnal nature and to the prevalent philosophy of the world where too often is found a selfish "me and mine" attitude.

In Exodus 30:37-38, God instructs Moses concerning the sweet spices and incense that were to be used in the tabernacle worship. The last verse of the chapter warns against using the perfume for personal use. A person who does, God says, will be cut off. Is it possible that we become intoxicated on the splendor of God's eminence? Perchance, do we grow heady as we participate in the glorious aspects of the church? Do we perfume ourselves with the grandeur and fail to give God the credit?

A holy attitude demands me to recall that the work in Rialto was built on the foundation another had laid and to understand that without that preexisting footing it would have been impossible to accomplish the small bit we did. There were other ministers involved, but I need to name Rev. Alice Anderson who labored there for many years, often under adverse circumstances, and who essentially established the work. Rev. Murray Layne, during his time as pastor, located and purchased the strategically located eight acres and began the construction of the beautiful auditorium building.

The Way of Holiness also may lead through sharp crannies where vision fails and where glittering dreams shatter. There came a day when Jerry was struck by a drunk driver, subsequently spent five months in a hospital, and then retired from pastoring. (That complete story is told in *A Thousand Pieces.*) However, the Way of Holiness is as sure and as safe during reverses as it is in the middle of the brightest and most productive days. The reason? God walks there. Always.

It does not depend on circumstances, nor on the way we feel. It does not matter how weak or strong we are or how young or aged we may be. It is imperative, then, that we keep a righteous attitude regardless of our situation. When fear stalks as surely as midnight beast, let us even more carefully walk. When our way seems a mere stretch of gauze pulled thinly over a vast chasm, and when the howling wind of failure and old age and death blow, yet we walk on. God will be there. God is there. I assure you, He is. I have tested the matter and found it so.

My walk in the Way of Holiness causes me to salute Rev. Larry Booker, the current pastor of the church in Rialto. Under his leadership, there has been tremendous growth, and plans now are being drawn for yet another building. He is the pastor of our only daughter, Rebecca, and of her son, Nathaniel, and though we, as her parents, introduced her to the Way of Holiness, a caring pastor is crucial for her continued safe journey. Rev. Booker is such a man, and in addition, he is an unusually talented preacher.

The Holiness Walk develops the spirit of a peacemaker, and although sin is not to be tolerated, and sin absolutely will keep us from the presence of God, a holiness attitude causes us to be longsuffering and to avoid being overly judgmental. Proverbs 19:11: "*The discretion of a man deferreth his anger; and it is his glory to pass over a transgression.*" How unusual! Pass over another man's transgression? On the contrary, perhaps we are too quick to turn from the Highway of Holiness so that we can readily share an observed infraction.

Look into Numbers 13:30, and consider Caleb's reaction when, as usual, the Israelites were complaining. The scripture says Caleb "*stilled the people.*" Chapter 14, verse 24 gives the reason for his success when it says Caleb had "*another spirit.*" Let us who are walking the Way of Holiness also have "another spirit," the spirit of godliness and of righteousness. Let us be humble and forgiving, and though never excusing sin, be tolerant of flaws and shortcomings in our fellow man. For in fact, when we see God, it surely will humble us, and we will recognize anew how truly unholy we ourselves are. Then we can say with the prophet Isaiah, Chapter 6 verse 5: "*…Woe is me! For I am undone; because I am a man of unclean lips, and I dwell in the midst of a people of unclean lips; for mine eyes have seen the King, the LORD of hosts.*"

HOLINESS EFFULGENCE

"*Who is like unto thee, O LORD, among the gods? Who is like thee, glorious in holiness, fearful in praises, doing wonders?*" (Exodus 15:11).

Extending far beyond the rules and regulations of what many term "holiness" is the brilliant radiance of God and the bliss and wonder of being connected to Him and to His majesty. While God will not share His glory with another, those who walk with Him are in some mysterious way permitted a glimpse, an ethereal brush, with His wonder and with His glory. In an unfathomable way, we enter into His mystery, an inscrutable, indescribable place. I love the words of Job in chapter 29 verses 1-4; a few of them are printed here. "*...Oh that I were...when the secret of God was upon my tabernacle:*" Have you been there? Have you somehow pressed into the very presence of God, into the Shekinah? Have you dwelt there for a time when the world fell away, and you were transported into another sphere? Did you ever try to tell someone about that experience, and, even as you spoke, you knew you could not explain it? A blank stare was returned or a shy grin or a knowing expression that affirmed, *you can't say it—don't even try. It is a useless endeavor; there are no fit words.*

Job was right—it is a secret, without earthly understanding and wholly unaccountable. When I speak of being in the presence of God my lame tongue stammers, its flawed words dissolving as does filmy steam cast into frigid air.

Consider these scriptures that speak to the glory, power, and majesty of God.

Jeremiah 50:46: "*At the noise of the taking of Babylon the earth is moved,...*"

Job 26:14: "*Lo, these are parts of his ways: but how little a portion is heard of him? But the thunder of his power who can understand?*"

I Timothy 6:16: "*Who only hath immortality, dwelling in the light which no man can approach unto; whom no man hath seen, nor can see: to whom be honour and power everlasting. Amen.*"

Numbers 23:21: "*...the LORD his God is with him, and the shout of a king is among them.*"

Luke 9:29: "*And as he* [Jesus] *prayed, the fashion of his countenance was altered, and his raiment was white and glistering.*"

Luke 9:32: "*But Peter and they that were with him were heavy with sleep: and when they were awake, they saw his glory...*"

Exodus 13:21: "*And the Lord went before them by day in a pillar of a cloud, to lead them the way; and by night in a pillar of fire, to give them light; to go by day and night:*"

Exodus 19:16-18: "*And it came to pass on the third day in the morning, that there were thunders and lightnings, and a thick cloud upon the mount, and the voice of the trumpet exceeding loud; so that all the people that was in the camp trembled. And Moses brought forth the people out of the camp to meet with God; and they stood at the nether part of the mount. And mount Sinai was altogether on a smoke, because the LORD descended upon it in fire; and the smoke thereof ascended as the smoke of a furnace, and the whole mount quaked greatly.*"

Exodus 24:16-17: "*And the glory of the LORD abode upon mount Sinai, and the cloud covered it six days: and the seventh day he called unto Moses out of the midst of the cloud. And the sight of the glory of the LORD was like devouring fire on the top of the mount in the eyes of the children of Israel.*"

Acts 9:3: "*And as he* [Saul] *journeyed...there shined round about him a light from heaven: And he fell to the earth, and heard a voice saying unto him, Saul, Saul, why persecutest thou me?*"

Scripture is replete with spectacular accounts of holy, supernatural acts of God that are quite past human perception. Let me emphasize the astonishing fact that when we walk with Him along the Way of Holiness, we absolutely enter into His power and mystery. Let us take another quick look into the second chapter of Acts, verses 1-4. "*And when the day of Pentecost was fully come, they were all with one accord in one place. And suddenly there came a sound from heaven as of a rushing mighty wind, and it filled all the house where they were sitting. And there appeared unto them cloven tongues like as of fire, and it sat upon each of them. And they were all filled with the Holy Ghost, and began to speak with other tongues, as the Spirit gave them utterance.*"

Seeking a natural explanation for that Pentecostal experience is as futile (and foolish) as trying to stuff a lightning bolt into a straw bag. No human mind can reason it, no rationalization can stand, and there is no thought that will clarify its meaning—that is, as far as human understanding and intellect are concerned. These are things of God, of the Spirit, wondrous, glorious, mysterious—available only to those who walk the Way of Holiness

At the public library in Chula Vista, as I worked on this chapter, I came across a small book entitled, *The Small Sects in America*, published by Abingdon Press. The insulting and ridiculous remarks that follow are found on page 97 of that book.

"*Under all these circumstances the cerebro-spinal system becomes highly excited, and the nervous energy thus generated or liberated in excess expends itself, as indeed it must in persons of low culture who lack rational control, in muscular movements. The emotions stirred in the revivals are those of fear, hate, and joy, the most powerful feelings known. Persons given to such reactions as those being discussed are nearly always the ignorant, in whom the lower brain centers and spinal ganglia are relatively strong and the rational and volitional powers residing in the higher centers of the cortex are relatively weak. Rational control is never marked in such individuals and it completely vanished under great emotional excitement. They are reduced to something like a primitive mental and nervous condition. Impulsive feeling rules. The stimuli never reach the higher centers, but are stopped by the lower centers and shunted immediately to the muscles. In the cases of glossolalia the subject breaks out in speech which is entirely divorced from thought, resulting in the jargon of unknown tongues. Jerks and the other muscular contortions are similarly explained.*"

I was astounded as I read this, as the author scorned the demonstration of the power of God and audaciously attributed these manifestations to the ignorant and to those having weak brains and who lack in rational power. Has this investigator of revivals not read the second chapter of Acts? Did he not study the actions of the apostles of Jesus Christ as they spoke with tongues and where their physical actions caused them to be thought drunk? Or rather, did he actually read and summarily lump together those godly men and women of yore with the rest of us who have experienced the phenomenon of the infilling of the Holy Ghost? His scorching, insulting remarks logically lead to branding the apostle Peter and every other Pentecostal preacher and believer as ignorant, weak minded, and of low culture. Rather strange (and probably evil)!

Please compare those fallacious remarks with the following incidents that graphically demonstrate the authentic glory and power of God. In the year of 2002, as I sat in a church in Colton, CA., I heard the pastor tell of an occasion when at the conclusion of a service in that very church, a lady named Mary approached the pastor and asked, "Does anyone here speak Greek?"

It was a small church, and Pastor Ted David was able to know and to tell her, "No, there is no one here who speaks nor understands Greek."

Mary was astonished, stared at the pastor, and persisted. "But someone who sat behind me in the service definitely spoke Greek. In perfect, scholarly Greek, as though spoken by one highly educated, the person extolled the greatness and power of God!"

Before including these details in this book, I called Rev. David to confirm them, and as we talked, he told me of his Syrian grandfather who in 1912 came to America. He received the Holy Ghost after arriving here, and in his circle of Syrian friends were some that were skeptical of his experience. He persuaded these people to go to church with him, and as they sat in the service, one of the women who had come with him leaned over and said, "Did you know that Jesus is God?"

"Why yes, I have learned that here," he replied.

"Did you know that Jesus is the flesh of God?"

A common English-speaking person under the influence of the Holy Ghost had spoken forth these wonderful truths of God—in a fluent Syrian language.

At the general conference of the United Pentecostal Church held in September 2002 in Phoenix, AZ., Rev. David Shatwell went early one morning to the prayer tent which was pitched on the paved area near the main entrance of the America West Arena. An Episcopalian priest was there also, having developed an extreme hunger for the infilling of the Holy Ghost. The two men talked together, then Rev. Shatwell prayed for the priest, who quickly received the Holy Ghost and began speaking in tongues. Further conversation revealed that the priest recently had been transferred and that the location of his new assignment would be thirty miles from where Rev.

Shatwell is the pastor of the United Pentecostal Church in Okemah, OK.[15]

You may think this to be co-incidence: I choose to believe that God is profoundly involved in the affairs of man, and that He supernaturally placed these two men together.

In an evangelistic campaign in Thailand, for convenience of prayer at the conclusion of the service, it was necessary to divide the people into groups of fifty. Rev. Jack Cunningham was one of several preachers who prayed for one of these groups. Once, as he finished praying, one of the ladies stared hard at him, rubbed her eyes, and seemingly in fear, backed away from him. Rev. Cunningham did not know what to make of this, but hers was such a strong reaction that he went to the pastor to ask if he had done something wrong.

"Did I frighten that lady? Is she afraid?"

"No," the pastor replied. "She is not afraid. That lady is forty-one years old, and she was just filled with the Holy Ghost."

"She was born blind," the pastor continued. "But, now she can see!"

At the very moment that she was filled with the Holy Ghost, she was completely healed of her blindness.[16]

Around 9:00 on a Thursday evening, October 3, 2002, Jerry and I received a telephone call from our eldest grandson, Christopher. "Granny, I'm getting ready to be a daddy." At that moment, he was in the hospital, where Christina would have her baby delivered by Cesarean section. A few minutes after 11:00 that night, the tiny baby girl was born, and I must tell you she is beautiful, looks like Chris, and her lovely name is Sage Loren. As become doting great-grandparents, we packed a few clothes, grabbed the presents we had prepared for this time, and on Friday, we drove to the hospital in San Diego. Sage lay in swaddling clothes, and in becoming, regal style, she received the beaming members of her family.

Our eldest son, Steve, who is the grandfather of Sage, pastors Hilltop Tabernacle in the San Diego area, and of course on the subsequent Sunday morning, we went to his church, joining with Sage's grandmother Dearrah and with other family members. Just after noon, Sage, along with her mother, was discharged from the hospital. Chris and Christina strongly felt that the church should be the first place Sage should go. Chris had arranged this with his dad, and after the morning service was over and nearly everyone had left the auditorium, we family and a few friends waited around until they could get there.

At the hospital, Christina's parents picked up the little family and then drove them to the church. Christina was pale as she walked down the aisle wearing fuzzy slippers and a long, black lounge dress. Chris walked beside her, looking a bit frazzled, wearing a simple tee shirt and jeans. In his hands swung a carrier; residing within was Sage. With wan smiles, the mom and dad walked to the front of the auditorium, and we gathered around them. Chris had lifted Sage from the carrier, and his other arm was about Christina.

We all cried, I believe, as we spoke simple prayers of guidance and direction, direction for us and for her parents, of health for the family, for wisdom and protection, and for long lives. We dedicated Sage to God—gave her back to her Creator, to the one who had given her life.

We stood on the Way of Holiness that early Sunday afternoon—a glorious, sparkling, mysterious way. Stretching ahead in a long line shimmers a heavenly convoy; in front, marches our incomparable leader, the majestic Lord Jesus, followed by godly fore bearers and those other saints already crossed over. Now here we stand in the line, as behind us our own godly children move into place, followed by our children's children, and now by Sage. It is a glorious way, this Way of Holiness, intangible and light, distinctly leading through this world but ending in an ethereal region, an otherworldly and rarefied place where finally we will know absolute peace, contentment, and everlasting joy.

ENDNOTES

[1] Plato, "Republic" in The Book of Virtues ed. William J. Bennett New York: Simon and Schuster, l993. 17

[2] J. R. Miller, Come Ye Apart London, Edinburgh, New York, Toronto and Paris: Thomas Nelson and Sons

[3] Barnes Notes Electronic Database Copyright 1997 Biblesoft n pag

[4] New Unger's Bible Dictionary Electronic Database Biblesoft n pag.

[5] Jamieson, Fausset, and Brown Commentary Electronic Database Copyright 1997 Biblesoft n pag.

[6] Keil and Delitzsch Commentary on the Old Testament New Updated Edition Electronic Database Copyright 1996 Hendrickson Publishers, Inc. Biblesoft n pag.

[7] Information taken from http://www.nps.gov/natr/index.htm

[8] Scott, Walter "Personality Parade" Parade 12 January 2003: 2.

[9] Lionel B. Fletcher, "Life Quest and Conquest" in Knights Master Book of New Illustrations ed. Walter B. Knight Grand Rapids: Wm B. Eerdmans Publishing Company, 1956. 386

[10] C. S. Lewis Letters to an American Lady, ed. Clyde S. Kilby. Grand Rapids: William B. Eerdmans Publishing Company, 1967. 19

[11] Charles Swindoll, The Finishing Touch Dallas, London, Vancouver, Melbourne: Word Publishing, 1994. 7

[12] Watkins, Carlton. Sermon. Hilltop Tabernacle. Chula Vista, Ca. 6 Oct. 2002.

[13] Hall, J. L. "In Appreciation of Holiness." Pentecostal Herald Feb. 2001: 10

[14] "Gospel Herald" in Knights Master Book of New Illustrations ed. Walter B. Knight Grand Rapids: Wm. B. Eerdmans Publishing Company 1956. 312

[15] Cunningham, Jack. Sermon. United Pentecostal Church General Conference. Phoenix. Sept. 2002.

[16] ibid.

AFTERWORD

It took only 21 days to get to Baghdad. As I concluded my work on this manuscript, the United States of America was living through momentous and startling times. Demonstrators in our streets were shouting their opposition to the war activities, while brave young men of the Coalition were fighting for the Iraqis—and for us. Indeed, military personnel from around the world fought and died so that freedom to speak out could continue in America, and that such freedom would be extended to the Iraqi people. My own nephew, Tim Forrest, was among those wounded, as artillery fire knocked him completely out of his vehicle, a military Humvee. He was taken to a hospital in Kuwait, spent several days recuperating, and then rejoined his troops. He is a Special Forces member of the 82nd Airborne. Today, I honor him and all other members of the Armed Services.

A man who did not understand his "road conditions" is Mohammed Saeed al-Sahhaf, the Iraqi information minister, who now is said to be on "administrative leave." "Wearing a constant smile and armed with fluent English and Arabic, he held court daily in front of dozens of reporters as the Iraq crisis intensified. He bemused the West with his litany of claimed victories over coalition troops."[1] Recall with me some of his greatest lines:

"My feelings—as usual—we will slaughter them all."

"We went into the airport and crushed them. We cleaned the whole place out. They were slaughtered."

"They have started to commit suicide under the walls of Baghdad. We will encourage them to commit more suicides quickly."

And the day before Baghdad fell as the troops were storming in…

[1] Taken from: www.miami.com/mld/miamiherald/news/world5625922.htm

"They're not even (within) 100 miles (of Baghdad)."

We smile easily at the antics of al-Sahhaf and laugh at his foolishness. That someone could be so dishonest with himself and with others is hard to comprehend: with no difficulty, we see how wrong and misguided is this man. Unconfirmed radio accounts report that when the web site http://www.welovetheiraqiinformationminister.com was initiated, it was receiving 4000 hits a second. There we buy tee shirts and barbecue aprons and cups that say, "No American will ever pour coffee from this mug! Never!"

A road is not pure mathematics, and cannot always be easily measured. Insightful was the Greek philosopher, Heraclitus, who said, "You can never step into the same river twice." In like form, I submit that one cannot walk twice the same road. Paper maps may show the distance to San Francisco as 350 miles or as 7000 miles to Baghdad, with the routing lines clearly marked. An understanding of the highway system may be complete and accurate, yet the driving conditions on any given road will vary considerably from day to day, demanding extreme caution and carefully honed skills.

Yet, physical roads are easier to maneuver and to understand than are roads of the Spirit and roads of the psyche. There are those who continue to be distracted and confused, often refusing to acknowledge the treacherous path they walk. The "Road of Life" is the most challenging of all. It constantly changes, and is fraught with both real and perceived danger. These roads are less sure than are physical highways, and sometimes they are not easily gauged.

The answer is clear, and with all confidence, I point to the Master Leader. I once more recommend the words of the apostle, Mark: "*He* [Jesus] *took the blind man by the hand, and led him out of the town.*" (Mark 8:23).

ABOUT THE AUTHOR

Shirley Buxton was born into the family of a minister, and thus, from childhood, she was reared in a Christian atmosphere. Jerry, the love of her life, is also a preacher, and they have been married now for 47 years. It is a tremendous joy to her that two of their sons and one grandson have also been called into the ministry. The work of God has been, and continues to be, the theme of her life.

The Buxtons have one daughter, three sons, eleven grandchildren, and four great grandchildren. Before her husband took his first pastorate, he served as a traveling evangelist. She, of course, accompanied him, making her own contributions to his ministry. Subsequent to that, Gerald pastored two churches, both in southern California, for a total of 34 years. Shirley thrived on being the wife of a pastor and was thoroughly immersed in their church work. She was totally supportive of her husband's ministry and helped him in numerous ways. She assisted with counseling, taught classes and home Bible studies, led ladies prayer meetings, wrote and directed dramatic presentations, and was closely involved with the music ministry of both churches. For several years, she was the administrator of New Life Academy, a Christian school founded by her husband. In 1996, Gerald retired from pastoring, and since that time, they have traveled extensively. Gerald has not retired from preaching, and Shirley continues to complement his ministry.

For more than 20 years, Shirley has been involved in the Ladies Ministries of the Western District of the United

Pentecostal Church, Int. She is the immediate past president and continues to be closely concerned with its functions.

Since early childhood, reading and writing have been an integral part of Shirley's life. In high school, she won awards, both for writing and for speaking. It was in the early years of her married life that she began to have her writing published. For several years, she wrote on assignment for Word Aflame Press. Two years ago, she wrote her first book. It has received excellent reviews.

Shirley tremendously enjoys entertaining, and the Buxton homes have always been centers of Christian fellowship. They reside now in Crestline, CA., a small town that sits 5000 feet high in the San Bernardino mountains. Her happiest days are when her family and friends come to visit.

A THOUSAND PIECES

"A powerful, emotional, faith building story of one man's struggle for life."

—Pentecostal Publishing House

"The gripping, true story of tragedy transformed into triumph! Not just another "my story" book, but the chronicle of a modern miracle of love and courage."

—Advance Ministries

"The author writes so well that you will not be able to put this book down!"

—The Library Builder

"What I appreciate most is your honesty and openness. Get it out there—it's needed."

—AWP Ministries

"*A Thousand Pieces* is indeed the best. Your faith will mount and your vision experience the miraculous as miracle after miracle unfolds. This is a book that shouldn't sit idly in your library, but should be passed on to uplift the power in the name of Jesus."

—Elaine Hogan, M.Ed., pastor's wife Phoenix, AZ.

"What an incredible account. I sat transfixed by the story that unfolded. Beautiful.

—Sharon Welch, South Dakota Ladies Ministries President, award winning artist, speaker

"I really think to be fair to your readers the cover of *A Thousand Pieces* should have a warning on it—Caution: May be hazardous to your sleep. Do not begin reading this book in the evening. Sunday night I decided to read a chapter or two before retiring for the night. I couldn't put the book down until 1:00 am. I finished it today."

—Rev. E. Simmons, Sr. associate pastor Revival Tabernacle San Diego, CA.

"It is powerfully written and inspiring faith and trust in God."

—B. J. Wilmoth, pastor Redlands, CA.

"I was a little angry at you when I read *A Thousand Pieces*. I found myself extremely exhausted because I could not put the book down."

—Walter Moore III, pastor Parker, AZ.

"Don't even start this book unless you're ready to laugh and to cry..."

—Edward Cantu, pastor Monument, Colorado

"...a beautifully written ...story. These passages are literary masterpieces..."

—Donald O'Keefe, author, pastor Pittsburg, CA

TO REORDER OR TO FIND OUT ABOUT
OTHER GREAT BOOKS BY FORREST PRESS,
PLEASE VISIT US AT:
WWW.FORRESTPRESSUSA.COM